Pr
MONEY

"Steven and Corinna Essa have written a masterpiece for creating money on demand. It's simple, proven and more importantly, highly effective and it's a guaranteed formula for creating cash for you. By implementing their systems, I'm able to bring in an additional $30,000 a month into my business."

– Pat Mesiti
Best selling author and international speaker

"Steven and Corinna Essa have written a must-read for anyone looking to leverage the power of the internet and webinars to generate money-on-demand. This book is full of actionable business and marketing advice, which I've personally implemented and resulted in sales of $5 Million Dollars."

– Mal Emery
"Millionaire Maker" and entrepreneur

"Anyone who is serious about generating real wealth consistently thanks to the Internet should read this book.

I have seen Steven pluck complete strangers out of a crowd and help them earn $2,000 to $22,000 online in 90 minutes or less. This strategy works."

– Mark Anastasi,
author of the New York Times bestseller
'The Laptop Millionaire'

i

"Steven and Corinna Essa are a very genuine couple for whom I have the utmost respect and trust. I know that they have changed the lives of thousands of people around the world by sharing their digital marketing skills.

I give them and their book my highest recommendation."

– Greg Owen
CEO - GOKO management

"There's a reason I work with Steven and Corinna Essa for promoting and putting on webinars and presentations: they are the best at what they do -- it's that simple. This book is a must read."

– Harry Dent
New York Times best selling author and economist

"Steven and Corinna really know how to do it.

Not only do they give you the specific tools you need to do your own webinars, theyshare the specific settings to get optimal results.

Using Steven's techniques I was able to pull in over $30,000 in sales on my first webinar.

I highly recommend this book for any budding online entrepreneur. The potential market out there is infinite.

I wish he wrote it ten years ago!"

– John Thomas
CEO & Publisher 'The Diary of a Mad Hedge Fund Trader'

"If you want a complete money-making business model laid out for you - here it is. In fact, 16 different... and brilliant... business models. I predict that as you read this book your mind will overflow with incredible ideas. You'll become very excited and find it hard to focus on the next chapter. That's how good it is. And even better, you'll know step-by-step how to do whichever model you want to follow. Brilliant stuff Steven and Corinna."

– Brett McFall,
The Presentation Guy, www.BoomerangBootcamp.com

"I have watched Steven and Corinna create incredible results for the clients that I have asked them to look after for me. There is no doubt that if you are looking for true masters using this powerful marketing medium, then look no further, you have found them."

– Ian Marsh
CEO Streetsmart Business School

MONEY

ON

DEMAND

The **16** Fastest Ways
To Becoming a **Millionaire Online**

STEVEN AND CORINNA ESSA

ISBN: 1542992893
ISBN 13: 9781542992893

FOREWORD

I became financially free by building online businesses that worked without me being there, without me having to be the expert, without me having to deliver customer support, or sell or anything else. The businesses are fully automated, with systems in place that run them and leave me free to do whatever I want.

This is true financial freedom—the ability to do what I want when I want, and on days that I don't want to log in to my businesses, the money keeps coming in.

In this book you'll see how I went from being over one million dollars in debt to being financially free—with multiple businesses generating tens of thousands of dollars a month on autopilot. In three short years I went from close to bankrupt to being a multi-millionaire. I don't have to work any more. I still teach because I love to teach, but I have more than enough money never to need to work again.

I used the Internet to make money to buy assets that generate me monthly income. Now I have businesses and property which pay me. The smartest, wealthiest people build a business for income, then invest in property, shares, gold/silver and other income-generating assets.

Every year my wife, Corinna, and I take off to Europe for their summer. I don't enjoy winter, and June to Sept is usually cold in Australia so we head to the Greek islands, France or Cyprus. Corinna and I wrote this book from the beautiful Greek islands. We hope you'll join us here one day.

I decided to take these three months to tell you my story and share my strategies. I wanted to share how in just a few short years, with no capital, no prior experience, no education degrees and no particular technical knowledge, I went from being broke and nearly bankrupt (thanks to bad real estate deals before the global financial crisis) to multi-millionaire.

I share how you can do this, too.

However, it's not enough just to acquire knowledge. You have to act upon it. I believe knowledge applied is power, and I trust that you'll find enough inspiration to take action on these strategies that have helped my clients, business partners and me to generate over fifty million dollars in sales.

Just remember, what's most important is to get started. Forget your perfectionism—perfect things as you go—like I did. Create the products after you've sold them! Never build a website until the business makes you money! Start with a webinar!

Good luck and enjoy the journey. I know I have.

Steven Essa

CONTENTS

INTRODUCTION

In the past few decades, technology has revolutionized every aspect of our lives, especially how we conduct business. Advances in the communication and technology industries have completely transformed the face and the pace of business in countless ways.

Information and files are now stored electronically, making access to information easier and faster than ever before. Emails, apps and social media have made communication instantancous. Wireless Internet and mobile devices have facilitated working remotely.

It therefore comes as no surprise that there has been a tremendous surge in 'web entrepreneurs', as barriers to entering the profession have almost completely disappeared.

Compare the costs of running a bricks-and-mortar business (five or six figure monthly expenses) with the costs of running a web-based business (as little as a few hundred dollars a month). It's not surprising that even teenagers now run their own niche businesses online! We've seen entrepreneurs as young as thirteen years old build their own audiences online—which they grow and monetize using platforms such as YouTube. YouTubers have become as big as TV celebrities.

We've seen successful business people completely abandon their corporate career to experience the 'laptop lifestyle'. We've witnessed stay-at-home mothers build a five-, even six-figure web business. We've also met people who've gone from incredible financial hardship to becoming millionaires thanks to the Internet and new technologies.

Why is this? Because web-based businesses:

- Cost very little in capital to set up and run
- An internet connection can cost as little as $20 a month
- Some email marketing services are free or cost maybe $15 a month
- Online conferencing tools are free or cost around $100 a month
- Website hosting doesn't exceed more than $15 a month
- Can use outsourcing to build teams for a few hundred dollars a month. Although this practice may attract some controversy, it allows companies to save up to 70 per cent in costs (Sharon Ottoman)
- Don't require offices—they only need access to a computer and internet connection
- Allow you to free up your time, as most tedious tasks can be automated or easily outsourced

Internet businesses have also become very attractive business models for various other reasons such as:

- Flexibility. You can work from anywhere, anytime you want, and as little or as much as you want
- No commuting. Having a web-based business puts an end to countless hours on the road, stuck in traffic

2

- Live anywhere in the world, such as a place in the sun, which is usually only an option for affluent retirees
- No office politics. A web-based business owner no longer has to put up with difficult co-workers, bullying or competitiveness
- No location restrictions. Anyone can find, communicate, interact and do business with people regardless of their geographic location

However, despite the many advantages of running an Internet business, not enough people have been able to reap the benefits of new technology. They've been too slow to adapt to these changes.

Too often, what stops people from experiencing the life and business described above is they simply don't know how to generate real wealth online.

Most courses currently available teach strategies that are extremely hard to implement and require too many resources. For example, a lot of web business educators teach people to sell information products for $27 to $47 by having a sales page online and driving traffic to that sales page.

This is a strategy that works, of course, and has worked for thousands of people. However, it can be tricky to implement for complete novices. Knowing how to drive enough traffic, day in, day out, to make the whole process worthwhile, is a difficult skill that only a few people have mastered. It requires skills in audience building, organic and paid traffic generation, excellent copywriting, and a good understanding of all tools and platforms needed to perform these tasks.

A few brave people will go ahead and try to master these skills. But there's so much information out there that it often just ends up paralyzing people even more.

In order to build a five-figure-a-month business with that particular strategy, you'd need to generate an average of 100 sales a month. When you consider that a sales page converts at one per cent at best (for every 100 visitors, one person buys), you'd need a total of 10,000 visitors a month!

This is why a lot of people who want to experience having a web-based business end up with shattered dreams.

That same frustration experienced by hundreds of thousands of people led us to discover an easier, faster way to monetize the Internet.

This strategy leveraged webinars. It was a strategy that didn't require as much traffic as websites to experience real profit. In fact, it's a strategy that only requires you to have ten people a week in order to generate a five-figure income a month!

Webinars are web-based seminars, allowing you not only to deliver information to hundreds—if not thousands—of people simultaneously and in real time, but also to sell to these same people.

What also makes webinars extremely powerful is their extremely high sales conversion rates. On average, webinars that are used to sell products and services convert at around ten per cent. Plus, because of the higher level of trust established with the webinar host during a one-hour long, live presentation, higher-priced products and services (as high as $15,000) are sold everyday.

4

And, based on these principles, anyone can experience the laptop lifestyle (yes, even complete novices)!

One single 90-minute webinar a week delivered to just ten people, which sells a $997 product (at a 10 per cent conversion rate) can generate $997 a week in revenue.

And it's thanks to webinar technology that many web-business millionaires have emerged—and many more are about to.

As for existing business owners, webinars offer them the ability to sell their products and services to anyone at any time with no geographic restrictions.

For example, a Sydney-based naturopath can, in addition to seeing ten patients a day face-to-face, deliver webinars to anyone around the world covering different ailments and their cures, and sell either additional information products, physical products such as food supplements, or even one-on-one sessions with people from remote areas. Webinars can now enable already established and successful business owners to remove their earnings-cap due to time and geographic restrictions.

Webinars have come at the perfect time—when most people prefer consuming information via video and feel comfortable purchasing online.

Both my wife Corinna and I have become financially free thanks to webinars.
I personally stumbled across that strategy, when, after completing a public speaking course I was constantly turned down by event promoters to speak on their stages, due to lack of experience.

My mentor suggested that I should get public speaking experience by delivering webinars, so I put together my first presentation, *How to raise money for churches and charities.* That very first webinar generated $594 in sales from just 15 people on the line.

It was at that moment that I experienced a breakthrough in my career and in my life. After trying to make a living from playing guitar in a band, panel beating, real estate investing and telemarketing, webinars changed my life. I currently own four multi-million-dollar web businesses in which 80 per cent of the revenue is generated from webinars.

Corinna, on the other hand, stumbled on webinars through her brother who shared my webinar course with her. Corinna studied my course, and put together a webinar selling a $997 product. Her first live webinar, in August 2011, generated a total of $15,952 in 90 minutes. This would have taken her more than a year to make, working 16 hours a day as an assistant television producer.

These days, our typical day looks like this:
We get up and exercise while admiring the view from our penthouse, which overlooks the beach. We check webinar registration statistics and answer emails. We then delegate assignments to team members. In the afternoon, I'll usually play golf for a few hours. Once a week I'll either deliver a live 90-minute webinar or attend a speaking engagement. We spend three months a year on Greek islands and travelling to places such as Thailand, Fiji and Las Vegas while our web businesses continue to tick over.

The good news is that the same opportunity is available for you today.

How?

The answer is WEBINARS.

This technology was recently only available to large corporations for thousands of dollars a year. Now it's available to anyone for just a few dollars a month.

Never before have you had the opportunity to sell products through live video conferencing to thousands of people simultaneously, from the comfort of your own home.

Imagine for a moment your life was like this:

- You live in or travel to exotic places, whenever you want, as often as you want without it ever affecting your level of income.
- You work just a few hours a day—sometimes only two hours a week—and have the freedom to do as you please.
- Your house is paid off, you have six figures in the bank and you're absolutely debt-free.
- You can forecast exactly how much you will or can earn next week, next month and next year because you have complete control over your numbers and therefore your earnings. In fact, for you, getting a pay rise is as easy as getting a few more people to your webinars.
- You're so financially secure—financially free—you're able to contribute to your favorite charity and make the difference you never thought possible.

The level of freedom and financial reward a webinar business can bring you is limitless.

Sean Allison, for example, was a divorced, depressed and broke government employee, struggling to pay the bills and stressed out to the point of exhaustion. He turned his life around thanks to webinars.

He came to one of my seminars looking for a way out of the hole his life had become. He had a few ideas he thought he could pursue with webinars. The first was teaching accountancy-related topics as he had studied accounting at university. The second involved health and fitness, as he'd previously been a personal fitness instructor. The third was teaching options trading as it had been his passion and he'd developed an effective method for generating cash flow from that strategy, and had helped a few people do the same.

I advised him to pursue the options trading idea, and within a year he'd generated over $155,000. Sean quit his job and moved from Perth to the Gold Coast to live by the beach. Why? Because he could now live anywhere. Four years down the road, his webinar business generates two million dollars a year. Twice a year he flies his whole family to his place for a beach holiday. He even spoils them from time to time with trips to Bali and Thailand.

Across the world in the UK, Dillon Dhanecha also attended one of my seminars. At the time, he was unemployed, thousands of dollars in debt and living off his partner's salary. Dillon happened to have extensive knowledge about Forex trading. He'd been successful trading the markets and had helped other people trade successfully. So, with my help, he put together a webinar teaching Forex trading. That single webinar generated £12,131 in 105 minutes. Within a year, his webinar business was making a million pounds and has been going from strength to strength ever since. He's now also known for his work in Rwanda, where his company The Change Studio invests thousands of pounds to fund young, innovative businesses. He also fulfilled his promise to his wife that she could quit her job to fulfill her dreams of pursuing a career as a freelance photographer. Dillon and his wife now travel around the world pursuing their dreams and making a difference in the world.

Would you like this freedom too? Would you like to make this sort of difference in the world?

Here's the good news:

Back when I discovered webinars, there was virtually no-one and nothing to show me the way. I had to work it out for myself. But today, there's a quicker way.

The plan is all laid out in this book in plain English.

This book shows you 16 different ways to monetize the Internet using webinars, regardless of where you are right now.
Regardless of whether you like selling or not.
Regardless of how introverted or extroverted you are.
Regardless of whether you are tech-savvy or not.
Regardless of whether you have a product or not.
Regardless of whether you have a mailing list or not.
Regardless of whether you have an idea or not.
Regardless of whether you have any experience in the subject or not.

In this book, you'll discover 16 simple ways to monetize webinars.

You'll have light bulb moments, one after the other...

You'll discover:

- How to build a million-dollar web business from scratch even if you don't have a product, mailing list or idea.
- How to turn your existing low-priced products into $2,000 or more products.
- How we took random seminar attendees and helped them generate from $2,000 to $22,000 in 90 minutes or less.
- How to automate your entire sales process thanks to the latest automation tools.
- Why you don't need to create a product before it actually sells (this means you get paid first, before you even have a product)!
- Why you don't necessarily need to create or even present a webinar in order to profit from one.
- The easiest and fastest ways to get other people to promote your webinar so you don't have to, and why you'll never have a lead generation or traffic generation problem.
- How people from all walks of life went from experiencing incredible financial hardship to becoming multimillionaires thanks to the strategies in this book.

My goal is, that when you finish reading the book, you'll have the keys to creating your own economy and live the life you've always dreamed of—and you'll be able to help others achieve the same.

OUR STORIES

Steven's Story

Since my early twenties, I was always on the lookout for something that would give me the financial freedom I was longing for.

I grew up in a family that lived on the single wage of a factory worker. Unlike many of my friends, I never went on vacation. I'd never even eaten at a restaurant until I was fifteen. From an early age, I remember thinking, "there must be a better way."

I loved music, and was convinced that the only way to break free was by producing a hit song, a song that would bring me the fame and money I needed to become financially free. So for thirteen years I worked very hard as a musician. I formed a heavy-metal band called *Cryogenic* and performed at big shows such as 'Big Day Out' which attracts over 50,000 people each year.

We decided to move to L.A. I remember living off the 99 cent store. I remember fighting with my band mates over a can of baked beans. Heinz baked beans were a treat for us, so if someone had a can, it would always lead to arguments. We even wrote our names on eggs so nobody else would eat them.

By the time our band was good enough to make it on the world stage, the music business had collapsed (thanks to music-sharing sites giving away music for free). One record label in L.A. told me, "You've come at the worst time." There was not much chance of us getting a record deal and making it in 2004. Morale was at an all-time low in the music business. The record labels resisted the Internet and tried to fight the changes, instead of thinking of creative ways to monetize the situation. Nobody had the creativity or vision of Steve Jobs from Apple who single-handedly took music online with iTunes and monetized it for artists and his company.

After struggling for thirteen years as a musician, still broke and in debt, I decided to give up. So after two years in L.A. I moved back to Sydney, Australia, which I thought, was the best country and city at the time. I left the music industry to go home and pursue financial freedom through building a web business and investing in real estate.

I listened to Robert Kiyosaki and Tony Robbins' tapes in the car during my lunch breaks, and I believed I was getting closer. I vividly remember when I heard Kiyosaki describe what "being in the rat race" meant.

Kiyosaki describes the journey of a person after they leave school. He talks about how they get a job, start making money and spend it all on themselves, on doodads and partying. Then they get married. Now they have two incomes to waste, so they buy a house, get two cars on finance, pay for vacations with their credit cards and live the good life. After their first child, the wife stops working or cuts her hours, so they're reduced to one income or less money but they have their big house. So the guy has to work harder or get a second job. Then the second child comes along, so they get a bigger house, and a bigger mortgage, and they have to work harder and harder and the rat race goes on.

Kiyosaki uses the analogy of someone running on a treadmill, and the treadmill is going faster and faster... and never stops. The whole time that family is sinking further and further into debt with no way out.

After listening to the tapes, I made the decision never to become that person. That was not going to be my life.

Soon after, I received a call from my friend Rony. He gave me a spare ticket to attend a seminar from the author of the book, *How To Make Money While You Sleep.* I didn't want to sacrifice a weekend to attend the conference, but I knew I had to, when two hours later a colleague of mine placed the book, *How To Make Money While You Sleep* on my desk and said to me, "Read this." Two different people recommended the same book in one day. I took it as a sign from the universe that I needed to attend this seminar.

Although I'd never enjoyed reading and had, in fact, never read a book from cover to cover, this one captivated me.

The author of the book soon became my mentor. When I saw him, when I listened to what he had to say, I believed that if I did what he did, I'd be successful.

My mentor taught me how to sell. He showed me the power of the right words to use when marketing and selling. But, above all, he conveyed to me the importance of putting together an irresistible offer.

When you have a product that people want and that people need, all you need is a platform from which to sell it. And the video-conferencing platform, also known as the "webinar platform" was the one I chose.

The first topic I ever presented on a webinar was, *How to raise money for churches and charities*. I invited a few of my friends and acquaintances, and fifteen people showed up to the live call. This webinar resulted in two sales at $297 in just 60 minutes.

My first $594 generated from this new technology was the beginning of my journey as the "go-to person" for selling with webinars. Over the past few years, I've trained thousands of people in how to create the life of their dreams using the Internet ... generating $10,000, $25,000, $100,000 or even $200,000 in under 90 minutes using webinars. Sometimes they did this without even speaking, selling or appearing on them—but more on that in a later chapter!

I've even run *automated* webinar campaigns that generated more than $90,000 in a few days.

I've travelled around the world sharing with thousands of people how to use web-conferencing technology to make a full-time living online. I've picked random people from the audience and implemented my Money-On-Demand formula using their knowledge base, and in hours we've generated thousands of dollars live in front of audiences.

My proven formula has so far generated over $50,000,000 in sales for my clients and my businesses.

Corinna's Story

I was raised and went to school in Greece. My dream was always to become a television producer. So when I finished school in Greece I left for London to study television production at the University of Westminster. I had dreams of working in TV. Those dreams were shattered when I discovered the very unstable nature of the industry and the myth of TV careers.

I did some odd jobs to contribute to my tuition fees, such as selling popcorn at a cinema, working as a waitress at a London hotel and working for a telemarketing company. I then got a job for a television production company APTV, covering the Greek Olympic games, and that's when I realized that what I'd learned at university was obsolete. The video editing software we were trained on at university hadn't been used for years by most television production companies!

I also worked for several television companies in London, Greece and France either as an intern or as a contractor. So I was either underpaid or looking for the next contract really soon. The last TV job I ever had was as an assistant TV producer at a Greek production company, producing TV commercials. I was working about 16 hours a day most of the time, from 10 am sometimes to 3am. I remember one night just sleeping on the couch in the corridor because it was too late to go back home, and I had to be back in the office a few hours later.

In spite of the long hours, everything was going well, I thought. I was given more and more responsibilities, which made me, believe I was there to stay. Unfortunately the financial crisis hit Greece very hard in 2009. Most companies started cutting salaries or, even worse, downsizing. I felt lucky because I escaped the first wave of redundancies in the company. However, a few months later, my boss called me for a meeting in his office where he said to me, "unfortunately Corinna, I don't have any openings for you at this stage. As soon as I do you'll be the first one to know." He never called me again.

Here I was, speaking three languages, with experience and a university degree and only entitled to unemployment benefits of 400 euros a month for 6 months. My rent was 700 euros a month. When I'd beg for any job opportunity, they'd smile at me, saying, "now is not a good time."

My story is very similar to thousands of people who were hit hard by the financial crisis. They either lost their jobs like I did, got their salary slashed in half, or experienced relentless rounds of tax rises. Unlike most people who still haven't recovered, I was lucky enough to be mentored through the whole process by my brother. He was—and still is—a very successful Internet business owner. He showed me the power of the Internet to create your own economy, how to generate income streams regardless of the government or market events.

Then I attended an Internet marketing seminar. I was excited, and I tried one of the strategies shared at that event. Soon I was making $700 a week selling products on Twitter!

At another Internet marketing seminar in London, a guy called Steven Essa happened to be speaking. We met ... and the rest is history. We were married nine months later!

I now own a multi-million-dollar social media marketing company in which 80 per cent of sales come from webinars.

CHAPTER 1

SHOW-AND-TELL

"Video is going to be the next big thing on the Internet," we often say.

When I first introduced the concept of selling with webinars at a conference in London back in 2009, no-one in the room had ever heard of that strategy.

At that same conference, a few speakers mentioned tele-conferencing as a means of selling products. However, with the introduction of high-speed Internet, it was obvious to me that video conferencing was going to take over.

A few months later, I received an interesting message from the seminar promoter of that event, who said, "Never before have I seen people become so successful as a result of a speaker's talk." Students and friends of his that had previously struggled to make any money online started generating $10,000, $20,000 or even $100,000+ online.

The months that followed the conference were very interesting. Testimonials came pouring in from people from all walks of life. They'd tried different strategies over the years without experiencing consistent results, and they shared how many sales they'd been able to generate thanks to webinars ... in a very short space of time.

The new 'web-conferencing' technology that internet marketers are now using, was, until recently, only available to large corporations at a cost of $100,000+ a year.

Thanks to the introduction of high-speed broadband internet, the price of video-conferencing technology has continued to drop, and people can now present webinars for up to 1,000 people at the same time, for just a few dollars a month!

The show-and-tell method is a very effective way to leverage your time. A webinar allows you to present to hundreds—or even thousands—of people at a time from anywhere in the world. In addition, the typical conversion rate of a show-and-tell webinar is ten per cent (compared to websites which usually convert at one per cent).

In other words, expect your webinar to convert one sale for every ten people who attend. If you're selling a $297 product, and 100 people are watching your webinar, expect to make ten sales, if not more.

In addition, webinars allow you to sell high-ticket offers priced at $1,000 to even $10,000, whereas it can be challenging to sell products for more than $200 directly from a website.

Show-and-Tell — step-by-step

1. Ensure your Internet connection has an upload speed of 0.85 megabits a second for the organizer. Speedtest.net is a great tool to use before presenting any live webinar, to check your Internet speed.

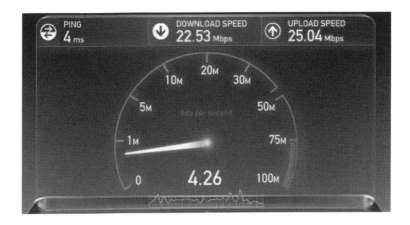

2. Buy a quality headset that includes a microphone and a mute button. The most popular one used on webinars is currently 'Logitech H390 USB headset'. This ensures that any background noise is removed, and should you be interrupted during the webinar for any reason—or feel the need to cough or clear your throat—you can simply click on the "mute" button.

3. Devise a catchy webinar title, also known as a "marketing hook."

19

It's important for the title to grab the attention of your target audience by giving them a big promise.

The title of your webinar will make or break the attendance rate of your event.

Examples of marketing hooks or webinar titles:

- Attention natural health practitioners: How to double your client base for free, thanks to the internet
- The little-known secrets to be back-pain-free naturally in 30 days
- The 7 natural remedies for arthritis
- Attention career women: 5 steps to getting the man of your dreams
- How to look 20 years younger naturally

4. Select the topic of your webinar

- Is your idea/topic grounded in personal experience? If it is, conveying your story on your webinar will give you all the social proof you need to convince people they should listen to you.
- Do you have passion or expertise in that field? Enthusiasm is contagious, so never present a webinar on a topic that you're not familiar with or have no particular interest in.

5. Understand who your target audience is.

Is your webinar targeted towards a healthy market? It's important that the target audience for your webinar has spending power, and is used to spending money in that particular field.

6. Come up with a great introduction

The first ten or fifteen minutes of a show-and-tell webinar are very important. Make sure that the introduction covers the following topics:

- Identify the webinar's intended audience.

    For example, imagine you're presenting a webinar on weight loss, titled *How to lose up to 5 pounds in 30 days and keep it off for good.* It's important you state specifically who the webinar is for.
    Based on the title, you might think the answer is obvious, but reiterating in more detail who the webinar is for, enables the viewers to identify themselves. The more you describe your target audience in detail and touch on their pain and challenges, the more they'll feel understood. This will impact sales.
    You should say something like,
    "This webinar is for you if you're a woman over 40 who has tried different diets over the years but as soon as you lose weight, you put it on again."
    Or,
    "This webinar is for you if you'd like to lose weight but don't have time to hit the gym."
    This is important because you want as many people as possible to say to themselves,
    "Great! This is for me, that's what I've been looking for."
    Or,

"Yes that's how I've been feeling, yes I hate the gym!"

- Describe who you are and why you're sharing this information.

"Why should I listen to you?" is a very common question and it's important that you answer it in the first ten or fifteen minutes of the webinar. Include as much evidence as you can that you have experience in the field. Show how you've achieved significant results yourself as a result of implementing the strategy that is about to be revealed in this webinar. This will establish that much-needed trust. And trust is a vital component for closing sales. As I always say, "nothing sells more than proof."

- Explain why the audience will benefit from this webinar.

To ensure your audience stays engaged throughout the whole presentation, make sure you whet their appetite with what's about to come. For example, don't give everything away by saying,
   "I'll show you that eating six small meals a day will make you lose weight fast without ever feeling hungry." It's best to keep a level of mystery by saying,
   "I'll reveal how you can eat more and still lose weight so you never feel hungry."

7. Make sure you structure the content in three, five or seven steps.

It's important that the content flows well, so the viewer feels you're taking them from point A (not knowing anything or knowing very little about the topic) to point B (having a clear understanding of how they can achieve the results promised in the title).

For example, the structure of your presentation could be:

Step 1: Set a goal and deadline
Step 2: Identify your bad eating habits
Step 3: Clear your fridge
Step 4: Prepare your weekly eating plan
Step 5: Keep a food diary

8. Illustrate the steps with stories and case studies.

Try to include in each step a story or case study to illustrate each point made. For example, talk about how your client, Lucy, identified that one of her bad eating habits was skipping meals because she didn't enjoy the meals provided at work. As soon as she realized that was making her store fat, she prepared her own lunch boxes and as a result lost five pounds in 30 days.

The more you include stories and case studies, the easier it will be for your audience to digest the information and remain engaged. Too often, presenters treat webinars as tutorials or lectures, which is the fastest way to lose your audience's interest!

9. Introduce your product or service.

To transition smoothly from the content to the selling, it's important to announce you're about to offer an opportunity for people to go further faster. A smooth transition could look like:

"If you've enjoyed this presentation and would like to learn more about how you can implement this strategy right now, I've put together a program called, *The weight loss fast track formula.*"

Alternatively, your transition could be,

"I've delivered priceless information to you, right? But if you haven't followed this system before, it could be a little overwhelming, right? Is it ok if I share with you how you can achieve your weight loss goals the fast and easy way?"

In the example above, you're simply asking permission to introduce your offer. Notice that you're asking a rhetorical question here and don't need to wait for approval. Because you've delivered quality information and content prior to the pitch, the majority of your audience will naturally want to learn more about how to progress faster or achieve results quicker! Remember that you're not selling them a product; you're offering a solution to their problem and helping them achieve an outcome faster through your product.

The example I often use here to illustrate my point is the drill. People don't buy a drill because they want a drill. What they want is a hole. They are buying the drill because they want to make that hole. With a weight loss product, they aren't buying your product, they're buying the body of their dreams.

CASE STUDY: ANNETTE DENSHAM

Annette Densham had never heard of the Show-and-tell method prior to attending one of our seminars. She'd been dragged to the seminar reluctantly, by a friend. Later Annette told me she'd only attended because the air conditioner at work wasn't working and she'd taken the day off work because it was too hot.

At 43, she'd recently been made redundant from a six-figure job and was working for twenty dollars an hour. She had twenty years' experience working in public relations and was looking for different options to turn her life around.

At the seminar, we conducted a competition, where I asked attendees to come onstage and share their ideas, for a chance to be coached one-on-one to implement the Show-and-tell method—and ultimately launch their business live onstage that weekend.

Out of around twenty people, Annette Densham won the competition. Her idea was to show people how to write a press release to get featured in the media. We turned her idea into a webinar titled *How to get a million dollars worth of free publicity.*

In less than 90 minutes, she showed the audience how anyone needing more customers could tap into the power of the media for free.

It's important to note that Annette didn't have a product, a website or a mailing list when she attended the event.

She then sold a $497 information course (to be delivered on future live webinars) on how to implement her strategies.

This resulted in $5,000 worth of sales in just under 90 minutes.

What's more, Annette hadn't even created the product yet!

That's another key point we teach students: don't create the product until you sell it—but more on that later in this book.

Annette now travels around Australia delivering her presentation at major networking events and mastermind groups, and has secured high-paying monthly clients who subscribe to her services as a result of this strategy.

CHAPTER 2

JV AND PARTNERSHIP

A Joint Venture (JV) is a collaboration between two businesses for the purpose of making money and tapping into each other's audiences. It is usually set for a short period of time, and allows businesses to profit from opportunities they might not be able to access individually.

The JV and partnership strategy is very fast and lucrative.

It involves marketing the webinar of a product owner for a 50-50 split of the sales generated. Of course, it doesn't have to be 50-50, but that's the usual split. If you have a physical product you can take out any costs first then split 50-50, there are no hard and fast rules here, so you can use your negotiation skills to get a good deal. Just make it a win-win situation.

The requirements are simple: the promoter should have access to a database of people who could potentially be interested in the topic of the webinar. (Later in this chapter, I'll look at how you get a "list" — a database of people.*)

For example, if the promoter has access to a database of authors, and the webinar owner has a presentation titled *How to become a New York Times bestselling author in 90 days* then the success of the joint venture is almost guaranteed.

Ideally, the webinar and product owner should have already tested the webinar and experienced a minimum of a ten per cent conversion rate. In such a case, the results of promoting the webinar through a JV partner are obvious. An accurate conversion rate can be calculated when a minimum of 300 people have watched the webinar.

Many video marketing and webinar replay apps and software products on the market, such as my own webinar automation software "Webinator.biz," allow you to track how many people have watched the webinar, when they leave, how long they watch for, if they click the 'buy now' button at the end, how many times they stop and start, which city they're in, what device they're viewing on and much more. What I love most about the Internet is that you can really make business predictable. You can track almost everything and can get rid of what doesn't work and keep what does.

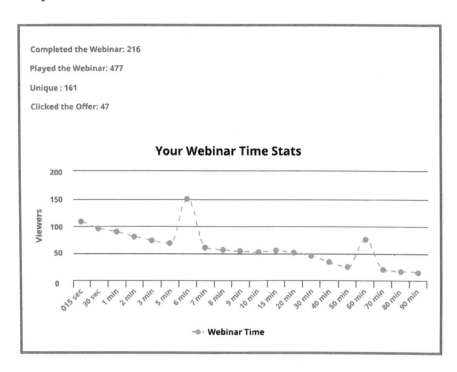

There are many platforms that allow promoters to connect with high-converting webinar owners. In this way, they can find high-converting webinars to promote.

The JV and partnership method is a devastatingly effective way to generate a five- or even six-figure income in as little as 60 minutes,

- Without having to own a product
- Without having to handle any customer support enquiries
- Without having to even deliver a presentation

It has proven to be a very successful strategy for marketers and database owners who wish to remain behind the scenes online while still profiting from the high revenues generated by webinars.

JV and partnership — Compounding success

1. Identify and contact a JV partner.
2. Schedule their webinar. When using a platform such as gotowebinar.com, the process is fairly straightforward.

   - You simply click on 'schedule a webinar',
   - Choose the time and date of the broadcast
   - Insert the title and the description of the presentation
   - Set the JV partner as the "panelist"
   - The JV partner will then receive by email the invitation to login to the platform at the time and date chosen

3. Promote the webinar so as to get as many people as possible to watch the webinar live or pre-recorded.

The most common ways to promote a webinar are by email, SMS and social media.

A typical webinar invitation by email looks like this:

Subject: New York Times Bestselling Author Reveals $30K Secret|

Hello (first name)

You need to jump on this quickly.
I mean it.
New York Times bestselling author **Mark Anastasi** is going to reveal on a LIVE webinar just for you:

How To Finally Attract The Wealth and Freedom You've Always Dreamed Of!

****

Option #1:
Tue. 5th May **8.30pm (Pacific)**
Tue. 5th May **10.30pm (Central)**
Tue. 5th May **11.30pm (Eastern)**
Wed. 6th May **1.30pm (Sydney)**
Click here to register for Option #1.
OR
Option #2:
Wed. 6th May **5am (Eastern)**
Wed. 6th May **10am (London)**
Wed. 6th May **7pm (Sydney)**
Click here to register for Option #2.

(When you click the link above, you'll be instantly registered for the webinar. There's no need to do anything else to register. Just click the link above.)
****

During the webinar he'll reveal:
- **How To Make $30,000 in The Next 30 Days.**
- The secret 'hidden' power that Millionaires and Multi-Millionaires tap into (and you don't!)
- **Why Tiger Woods, Tony Robbins, John Assaraf, and Joe Vitale achieve their goals.**
- 5 Steps to Finally Attracting The Wealth and Freedom You've Always Dreamed Of!
- **How To Get Your Life To Finally Take Off In 2017!**
- ... and much, much more!

Click here to register now (below).
****

Option #1:
Tue. 5th May **8.30pm (Pacific)**
Tue. 5th May **10.30pm (Central)**
Tue. 5th May **11.30pm (Eastern)**
Wed. 6th May **1.30pm (Sydney)**
Click here to register for Option #1.
OR
Option #2:
Wed. 6th May **5am (Eastern)**
Wed. 6th May **10am (London)**
Wed. 6th May **7pm (Sydney)**
Click here to register for Option #2.

(When you click the link above, you'll be instantly registered for the webinar. There's no need to do anything else to register. Just click the link above.)

See you on the webinar!

Sign off

P.S. This webinar is a one-off. Don't miss out! Click here now (below):

* *

How To Finally Attract The Wealth and Freedom You've Always Dreamed Of!

Option #1:
Tue. 5th May **8.30pm** (Pacific)
Tue. 5th May **10.30pm** (Central)
Tue. 5th May **11.30pm** (Eastern)
Wed. 6th May **1.30pm** (Sydney)
Click here to register for Option #1.
OR
Option #2:
Wed. 6th May **5am** (Eastern)
Wed. 6th May **10am** (London)
Wed. 6th May **7pm** (Sydney)
Click here to register for Option #2.

If promoting the webinar on social media, a simple announcement like the one below works quite well.

Steven Essa shared Steve Essa's photo.

Steve Essa

Really looking forward to hearing New York Times bestselling author, Mark Anastasi reveal on a live webinar "How To Finally Attract The Wealth & Freedom You've Always Dreamed Of!"

https://attendee.gotowebinar.com/regist.../2671926871388134146

Adding large pictures like the one above to social media posts leads to more engagement and enables you to be more visible on people's timelines.

SMS marketing has also proven to be extremely effective. Most people never part with their phone, and check it several times a day, so it's a great way to promote a webinar.

A typical SMS broadcast would be as short as possible and preferably personalized like the one below:

> Hi Mary, just wanted to let you know we're running a live webinar with New York Times bestselling author—about how to finally attract the wealth and freedom you've been dreaming of! Register here: http://tiny.cc/67goxx You'll be glad you did!

SMS marketing platforms exist in most countries and can be found by simply performing an online search.

4. At the time of the broadcast, the promoter will login and make the panelist an organizer so the audience can hear him and see his screen.

5. Introduce the webinar presenter (JV partner), especially if the audience is not familiar with them. This establishes trust.

   The introduction should be short, and underline why the audience should listen to the presenter. An introduction will typically sound like the one below:

   "Hello, and welcome to this webinar on how to double your business thanks to social media. And presenting this exclusive webinar, is Helen Smith. Helen has been a social media strategist for the past six years, has created over 500 successful social media campaigns for businesses around the world, and is the author of the book, *Social Media Marketing Secrets*. I can't wait for her to share her invaluable information. Over to you Helen."

6. Split the profits! On most occasions, agreements between the promoter and webinar owner are made

on a handshake and based on trust. Typically, the webinar owner will process payments and provide proof of the sales.

Alternatively, the webinar owner will create an affiliate account for the promoter who will be able to track the sales made through his affiliate link by logging in to his account.

Affiliate links and accounts can easily be created using platforms such as JVpro.com or infusionsoft.com

*Notes on building a list.

There are many ways to build a list. The most common ones are through solo ads, ad swaps, media buying or social media.

A solo ad means you pay a database owner a flat fee to email their list. Most database owners are happy to do this as it adds another income stream for them without them having to sell anything, plus it's an opportunity for them to email their list with quality content (the webinar).

Ad swaps are another very effective way to build a list. With ad swaps, a database owner will email his list in exchange for you emailing yours about his offer. No money is exchanged—it's based on reciprocity. There are many websites available that can put you in touch with list owners willing to be paid to email their list. A simple Google search for "ad swaps" will take you to all the different websites that offer this service.

Media buying is the process of buying advertising space on the Internet. There are plenty of ways to buy media on the Internet, either through Google advertising, banner advertising or social media advertising. Most advertising networks allow you to either 'pay per impression' or 'pay per click'. 'Pay per impression' means you pay a flat fee based on how many times your ad will be displayed. For example, you can pay a flat fee of $100 to show your ad 1,000 times. 'Pay per click' means you only pay according to how many times your ad has been clicked on. For example, if each click costs $2 and you've received 100 clicks, you pay $200. If, on the other hand, no-one has clicked on your ad, it doesn't cost you anything.

Social media is also a very effective way to build a list for free. Social media is free to join and most social media users have an average of 140 contacts. This means that if you have a social media presence, you most likely already have 140 contacts (if not more) that you can leverage to build your database. All you need to do in order to capture their name and email to grow your database, is offer them something for free in exchange for their name and email. For example, if you're in the dog training industry and would like to build a database of pet owners, you can offer a free dog-training lesson in exchange for someone's name and email. Although your social media contacts might not fit the mold of who you're trying to target, it's a good way to start—and if your free offer is irresistible, people can share your offer to their contacts, for you to benefit from 'word of mouth'.

CASE STUDY: MARK ANASTASI

Mark Anastasi (online entrepreneur, New York Times best selling author and my brother-in-law!) made $200,000 in sales in 90 minutes thanks to a webinar!

Mark writes:
Thanks to the JV and partnership strategy, I've generated millions of dollars in sales. When I decided to implement this strategy, I made a deal with an expert to deliver his presentation and sell his $997 offer to my audience. All I needed to do was *promote* the webinar, and we'd split the sales 50-50.

Five days before the webinar, I started emailing my subscribers about it and I got over 1,000 people to register for the event, which meant I could expect approximately 300-380 of them to show up for the actual webinar.

I wanted to get more people onto the webinar, as a webinar hosted on gotowebinar.com can hold up to 1,000 participants at the same time.

With time running out, I offered $1,000 to two joint venture partners of mine, for them to promote the webinar to *their* mailing list as well (see the information above about solo ads)! It would take them approximately five minutes to send out an email, and they'd each pocket $1,000 in pure profit. Not a bad deal for them. I even wrote the email for them, so they'd only have to copy, paste and send it. That's what you have to do for anybody who is mailing their lists for you. Do the work, make it easy to copy and paste, or they might not send it for you.

What *I'd* get in return would be exposure to over 500,000 subscribers on their combined mailing lists.

My $2,000 investment paid off. Thanks to this additional last-minute exposure **we got an extra 1,200 people registered** for the webinar, a total of 2,240 registrations.

More than 700 people from around the world watched the webinar *live* (and hundreds more watched the webinar *replay* the next day). My joint venture partner presented his content and offer, and achieved a massive $200,000 in sales in 90 minutes!

Note: Mark then set up a replay, allowing people to watch the webinar in their own time, which resulted in an average of $8,000 a month in additional sales—but more on that strategy later in the book!

CHAPTER 3

LAZY MONEY

A webinar is a powerful tool because of its ability to generate multiple passive income streams thanks to replays.

When the live webinar platform gotowebinar.com was first introduced, it enabled you to record your presentation only on Windows PCs and not on Apple Mac computers. And, when you'd recorded your presentation, it would produce a big clumsy .wmv file that wouldn't play online unless it was converted into an mp4 file first. Then, you had to use different software to make the file play on a web page.

This tedious process led me to create my own webinar replay system called 'Webinator'.

A webinar replay is a very smart way to leverage your time and earn multiple income streams on virtual autopilot.

It's common for audiences to register for a live webinar, but be unable to attend. Typically, about half to three quarters of the people who register don't show up for the live presentation. Now, thanks to replays, it's easy to email registrants the replay for a second chance to catch the presentation.

A standard webinar replay email looks like this:

Hello Judy,

What a fantastic webinar we had today. Over 674 people registered for "How To Generate Cash Flow In 30 Days Thanks To Social Media" and hundreds of people joined us live.

The feedback received was amazing! If you were able to join us live, congratulations!

As promised, we recorded the entire presentation and the replay is now available here:

LINK

During the webinar we revealed:

- How To Get Thousands Of **Targeted Fans and Followers** on social media!

- The **Little-Known Strategies For Monetizing** Social Media Right Now, Even If You're A Complete Beginner!

- How To Gain More Authority And **Grow Your Brand Fast** Thanks To The Viral Power Of Social Media

- How To Put Your Social Media Marketing **On Complete Autopilot**

- How You Can **Make Money** Thanks To Social Media RIGHT NOW Even If You Don't Have a Website, Product, List, Or Any Money!

- The Secret Code To Siphon **Unlimited Free Targeted Leads in 7 Seconds!**

- How To Capture Your Followers' Names And Emails In Just One Click And **Build A Huge List Fast**

... And much, much more!

Watch it now before it gets taken down: <u>LINK</u>

Just implementing one strategy will make a huge impact in your business and could potentially allow you to generate a few hundred bucks during the webinar!

Enjoy!

Corinna Essa

P.S. Just a few hours are left to watch the webinar replay before it gets taken down. Make sure you watch it now: <u>LINK</u>

Furthermore, the ability to provide replays also allows presenters to share their information to audiences around the world regardless of their time zones.

For example, should you wish to share your webinar with an American audience, only available in the evening—while you're based in London—it no longer means you need to do so at 1 a.m.!

Thanks to replay technology, your webinar can be available to anyone in the world regardless of time-zone differences,

41

and you can generate sales whether you get out of bed or not!

In other words, replays allow you to make your information and products available to anyone in the world, at any time, without investing any extra time and effort. Thanks to this technology, you simply work once when you deliver the live webinar and get paid over and over again for it!

To this day, we haven't come across a business model as effective as the webinar replay formula, where you can generate more income while doing absolutely nothing for it.

Lazy Money — Work once and get paid over and over again

Webinator, which allows you to automate your webinars, is a very simple software product. Once you've secured your copy at www.Webinator.biz, login to the software and follow the prompts.

It enables you to automate an unlimited number of webinars. In addition, it creates a web page that plays your webinar like the one below:

The Little-Known Social Media Monetization Secrets Revealed

What makes it even more powerful, is that it allows you to set up registration pages, where people have to submit their contact details before accessing the replay.

By capturing an audience's contact details, webinar owners can build a highly-targeted mailing list, which can be followed up if the customers don't buy immediately after watching the replay. They can also be contacted at a later stage for future offers.

An added feature of Webinator is its ability to hide the player controls. This means that viewers can play or pause the video but not rewind it or fast-forward it. That way, viewers are obliged to watch the whole presentation before judging the offer.

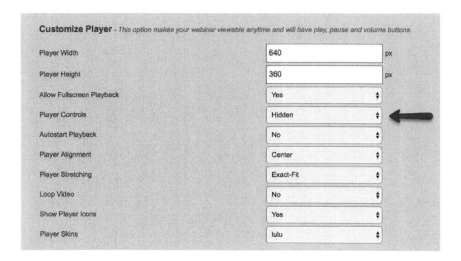

For a webinar to convert well, it's important that audiences watch it in its entirety in one sitting. In this way, they're taken through a carefully crafted process, and their appetites are whetted for more, before being offered a product.

What also makes Webinator an effective tool is its ability to make the "pay" tab appear only after the offer has been presented and the price has been announced.

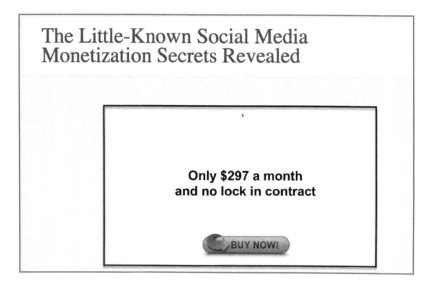

That way, when viewers watch the presentation and there is no "buy now" button below it, they don't jump to the conclusion that this webinar is just another sales video. They don't have their guards up.

Instead, they just consume the information as they would when watching an information presentation. Through extensive research, we've discovered that this method leads to higher sales conversions on both webinars and in video sales letters.

A webinar replay can also be available in three different formats when using Webinator. It can be available at any time (aka 'play anytime webinar'), or be available only once on a specific day (aka 'one time webinar'), or it can be available on every day or every week at a certain time (aka 'recurring webinar').

Setting up webinar replays to be available only on a specific day usually leads to higher conversions, because people will ensure they make themselves available to watch the presentation in full, knowing it won't be available again anytime soon.

Combining scarcity of the availability of a webinar with a highly committed audience is the winning formula for achieving higher sales conversions.

Webinator also provides you with the 'Embed code' of your replay, allowing you to replay the webinar on any web page such as your website or blog.

By adding a webinar replay to your website, not only can you build a highly targeted mailing list, you also have the opportunity to convert your standard website into a highly effective sales funnel.

CASE STUDY: SEAN ALLISON

It's not uncommon for webinar replays to perform better, in terms of sales, than the live version. This can be easily explained by the fact that, thanks to replays, audience members can choose the time to watch the webinar that's most convenient for them—or when they have fewer distractions.

When Sean Allison (an ex-government employee from Perth) first decided to use webinars to generate income—and potentially replace his income—he had three choices.

- He'd been a personal trainer for a few years and could have put together a webinar and product around the topic of fitness and weight loss.
- Another option was to put together a webinar about accounting, helping people save on tax for example because he'd worked as an accountant in the past.
- His third option was to put together a webinar on options trading, as he'd developed a passion for it.

He decided to pursue the latter as he was already using the strategy for himself while still working at a job, and had already shared his formula to friends and family who were experiencing considerable returns.

All he had to do was to package his knowledge and expertise into an information product. This led to the creation of *The Income Generator Strategy*, a product that sold initially at $997.

Below is an image of how his webinar replay outperformed his live webinar.

As you can see from the screenshots below, his live webinar, held on April 24, generated five sales at $997 between the hours of 8.20am and 8.45am.

4/24/2012 08:45:00 AM	Regular	Tina	$997.00
4/24/2012 08:29:00 AM	Regular	John	$997.00
4/24/2012 08:26:00 AM	Regular	Aleksandra	$997.00
4/24/2012 08:23:00 AM	Regular	Don	$997.00
4/24/2012 08:20:00 AM	Regular	Hugh	$997.00

A few hours later, when the webinar replay was shared with the registrants who didn't attend the live session, an additional 16 sales were generated from 1.17pm on April 24 and in the following days.

That's an additional $15,952 for doing absolutely nothing!

4/24/2012 11:09:00 PM	Regular	Alan	$997.00
4/24/2012 08:33:00 PM	Regular	Marilyn	$997.00
4/24/2012 04:54:00 PM	Regular	Mark	$498.50
4/24/2012 02:35:00 PM	Regular	Helen	$997.00
4/24/2012 01:17:00 PM	Regular	Jenny	$997.00
4/24/2012 08:45:00 AM	Regular	Tina	$997.00
4/24/2012 08:29:00 AM	Regular	John	$997.00
4/24/2012 08:26:00 AM	Regular	Aleksandra	$997.00
4/24/2012 08:23:00 AM	Regular	Don	$997.00
4/24/2012 08:20:00 AM	Regular	Hugh	$997.00

At the scheduled live webinar time, over 100 people tried to login. Since 100 people was the limit on attendance, a notification appeared saying, "This webinar has reached its limit of 101 attendees." This resulted in many people eager to access the information but unable to do so.

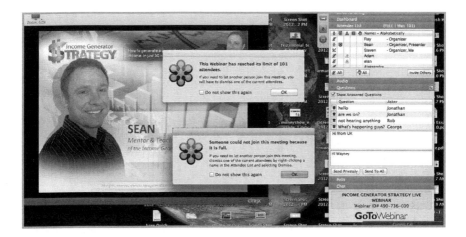

Sean used this to market the replay in an email to registrants, as a highly sought-after presentation. We were able to create genuine urgency in our follow-up marketing because many of the people who received the replay email, actually experienced the disappointment of being unable to attend live.

Sean went on to make millions of dollars from his webinar presentation and went on to create online information courses on options trading. He is now highly regarded for his knowledge and skills around options trading. His company now educates people all over the world and he employs more than ten people. He runs weekly live webinars of up to three hours for his high-level 'elite' students who pay him $10,000 or more per year for access to his information.

He also continues to sell his courses, retreats and personalized knowledge using webinars. Sean never creates a product until he sells it. He has built a multi-million dollar company using this model. He has followed my advice of not wasting time on something until someone has committed to paying for it.

Everyone I meet has a four to ten thousand dollars a month business in their head, using only the knowledge, experience, or skills they currently have. If they say to me, "I don't want to be the expert or put myself out there," then I say, "Do you know someone who is an expert and would like to get their message out there? Because they will most likely be open to sharing half their profits if you help them to share their knowledge and expertise with more people!"

CHAPTER 4

PARTNERSHIP

Four years into my life as a webinar expert, I was already making hundreds of thousands of dollars a year thanks to promoting my own webinars.

Throughout the years, many people had approached me, offering the opportunity to set up webinars for a fifty per cent share of the business. However, I declined all these opportunities as I was busy enough running my own webinar business.

As years went on, more and more people reported how much income they'd generated as a result of using my Money-On-Demand webinar system in their sales funnel.

All these people, not surprisingly, had one thing in common: they'd become quite busy in their own businesses. Most were making more money than they had in their entire life. They'd transformed their lives.

This is the most gratifying aspect of what I do. My number one goal is no longer to make money—although that may sound hard to believe from someone whose book is called "Money-On-Demand"—but making money is not what I'm the most passionate about. It's not my number one goal. My passion and top priority goal is to help free people from the rat race. It's to help businesses grow, to help 'solopreneurs' turn their ideas into income-generating assets. It's to help people become financially free by creating a successful Internet business.

To me a business is the most powerful way to make money, and with money you can control your destiny. With your own business, you're accountable. You're responsible. The buck stops with you. There's no one else to blame. When a business pays off (which it does one in ten times in traditional business) the rewards are huge.

I've been in my own business and working for myself for as long as I can remember—I was a paperboy, I did odd jobs in the neighborhood, I knocked on doors to wash cars and do maintenance for money. Then came my thirteen-year stint in the music business, which entailed more business lessons than all thirteen years of school before it. The music business taught me about business, about honoring my word (and the haunting pain it caused when I didn't). It taught me about hiring people, firing people, motivating people who work for nothing to help a bigger cause, dealing with retail stores for our branded t-shirts, negotiating with record labels, distribution, maintaining a fan club (which is known on the internet as 'list building'), marketing and all the rest. This prepared me, more than anything, to understand just how easy making money online is, compared to the music business I had experience in.

A small business owner works an average of twelve to sixteen hours a day.

Some of the tasks they have to perform on a daily basis include:

- Selling
- Customer support
- Administration

- Bookkeeping
- Hiring staff
- Managing staff
- Product creation
- Traditional marketing
- Web marketing (social media, blogging, webinars, etc....)

When so many responsibilities are imposed upon a business owner or expert, it's normal for some areas to suffer. In fact, many business owners and experts admit to being willing to give half their profits to someone who could handle the marketing side of their business.

Anthony Chadwick, for example, is a dermatology vet. He sold his practice after discovering the power of webinars, and now runs a multi-million-dollar business selling training to vets using webinars. He said he would have been willing to give half his profits to someone who could handle the webinar aspect of his business, if someone had offered to do this before he worked out how to do it himself.

I started asking the people who were doing webinars this question: if someone had come to you before you built this business, and they offered to build it for you for free but take a 50 per cent stake in the business—you just show up and speak—would you have taken it? The overwhelming response I got was a massive YES.

I asked myself why I didn't think of taking a share of their business, considering how many millionaires I'd made thanks to my Money-On-Demand system. I realized that if I'd just taken a ten per cent share in each business, I could have stopped coaching, training and selling my own programs and products and could easily have lived as a millionaire on royalties from the other businesses I'd helped build.

Unfortunately, at the time I started my business I didn't feel confident enough to ask for both payment for my program and a percentage of their business. That's not what I was taught to do. But since my programs and products were making so many people rich, I gained confidence and started to think outside the square. I began to see the bigger picture and the massive potential for passive income. Taking a share of someone's business was also a fantastic opportunity for the business owner to have me on their team. After all I'm the Money-On-Demand master!

After watching thousands of hours of webinars and critiquing them second by second, slide by slide, and writing and re-writing scripts for students, I'd mastered the art of selling on webinars. I can look at a PowerPoint presentation and tell you if it will be too long or too short. I can tell you if the product will sell by looking at the offer and I can even tell if they'll bore the audience to death or excite them. When you do something many, many times for years and years you just get good at it. There's no secret.

I studied and implemented everything I learned from my first mentor, Brett McFall, and then I took his information to the next level and duplicated my business model for a 50 per cent share of other companies I started from scratch.

Now I buy into companies who have experts and coaches. My wife Corinna and I just acquired 50 per cent of a company we bought for pennies in the dollar, and it has become a multi-million-dollar business. It was being mismanaged, losing thousands of dollars every month, but we'd seen the books and products that the business was selling and knew we could turn it around. Within four months it went from red to black, pulling in over $30,000 a month in net profit for us.

With so many people now profiting greatly from using webinars, a trend has emerged. More and more people want to introduce webinars into their marketing mix, and more importantly, are willing to give half their profits to someone who is able to set up and promote their webinars for them.

An expert or business owner is usually passionate about their area of expertise and is interested in sharing their information, services and products with as many people as possible. The idea of setting up, marketing and automating webinars is daunting.

As a result, a huge opportunity is emerging for anyone who knows how to set up, market and automate a webinar—to become a 'webinar facilitator'.

The income potential for a webinar facilitator is limitless. All it takes is scheduling a few webinars a month for the business owner, sending emails to market the webinars, and recording them. This doesn't take much more than two to four hours a week. In fact, a webinar facilitator can perform these tasks for up to ten businesses, and own fifty per cent of each business.

For each business, a webinar facilitator performs the following tasks:

- Schedules webinars
- Sends emails to promote the webinars
- Finds partners to promote the webinars
- Records and automates the webinars
- Checks the sales

In other words, the facilitator simply provides the platform for the expert or business owner to be able to sell more products and services—without doing the legwork.

There are currently more business owners and experts than there are facilitators. In fact the ratio would probably (as a rough estimation) be one facilitator for every 500 experts.

The advantage of becoming a facilitator, rather than a simple affiliate, is that you benefit from ongoing earnings. A typical affiliate deal requires you to promote a product owner for a one-off commission. The money generated from upsells and downsells never lands in your pocket, whether you generated the lead in the first place or not. Affiliates end up building the customer base of product owners, which is the most valuable asset of a business! Most profits are usually generated not from the front-end product, but the back-end ones.

BIG TIP:
The money in an online business is usually made from the back-end sales of higher-end products and services, not the front-end ones offered. Usually the front-end offer—what I call your 'main offer'—is what funds the business. It covers your day-to-day business expenses. The real profit is made on the back end—from what I call your 'Profit Maker' product. Businesses that try to make more money by cutting costs won't make more money. They'll annoy their customers, appear cheap, or they'll make their product worse or inferior. It's so much better to offer a done-for-you service, a high level/advanced product, a retreat, a bootcamp, a workshop, or whatever else the customers need to help them achieve their desired outcome faster.

Let's say you decide to promote a real estate investing course as an affiliate priced at $5,000, and for every sale generated as a result of your marketing, you make $2,500. Although this might sound attractive, considering the fact you don't have to deliver the product or handle any customer support, you're also kissing goodbye a $5,000 buyer. This buyer is very likely to buy the ongoing upsells and downsells of the product owner for years to come without you ever profiting from them.

Mark Anastasi (online entrepreneur, New York Times best-selling author and my brother-in-law!), who had been an affiliate for ten years, once confessed to me,
"I've realized I've just helped so many people build multi-million-dollar businesses as a result of me promoting them just once."
Thanks to the partnership model, you now can have a piece of the back-end sales too.

The partnership model is much more profitable and doesn't require you to produce more work. The prerequisite for you to promote an expert is simply for them to agree to give you a share of the entire business.

An expert who fits the criteria described above will gladly agree to this deal. He/she typically doesn't have access to a database, or they do and don't know it or don't know how to manage it. They may have no interest in building and managing a database, and therefore will happily give you a fifty per cent share of their business for providing that facility on an ongoing basis.

Why? Because it takes time. Experts are usually busy with the day-to-day tasks and responsibilities of running a business. Most business owners who are experts in their business never rest, and when they do, they feel guilty—for watching TV or going on holiday—they feel they have to be working all the time.

You're a breath of fresh air to them. The smart business owners who love what they do, love working with their customers and want to work with their customers are the only experts I want to partner with. If a business partner doesn't like or doesn't want to work with their customers, I walk away.

Why? Because who is going to work with the customer? Customer service is everything in a business—especially online. The experts have to focus on customer service and product satisfaction while we work on their marketing and building a product line and funnel that is both profitable and delivers great value and RESULTS for the customers.

Also, I'd never work with someone whose products do not get results for their customers. That won't be a long-lasting business. Your reputation must be your number one priority online. It's your biggest asset whether you're a big business or single person business.

In addition, it is a virtually risk-free model. Money is split only after all the costs of running the business have been deducted.

The typical recurring costs of such a business model are:

- Autoresponder service (about $15 a month)
- Website hosting (about $10 a month)
- Printing costs (depending on how heavily you rely on printed marketing material)
- Subscriptions (any subscription to newsletters or courses)
- Taxes
- Costs of sales (cost of delivering the product or service)

- Phone
- Internet
- Staff
- Events (if running events is part of the sales funnel)

This model is perfect for anyone who loves marketing, and more specifically, who loves the idea of earning a very good income while remaining behind-the-scenes.

To become a sought-after facilitator, it is absolutely vital to have access to a large, targeted list. There are currently many ways to build such a list. These are some of the most effective ways:

- Social media
- YouTube
- Banner ads
- Blogging
- Buying lists
- Cold calling
- Google ads
- Yahoo ads
- Conferences
- Networking
- Joint ventures
- Solo ads
- Ad swaps

From $1 million to $10 million

1. Look on Amazon.com or Youtube.com. Experts usually have books listed on Amazon or have videos of their talks and presentations on YouTube. Look at podcasts, go to events. People who already speak on

stage usually don't do much online, and have most of what you need to succeed. If you see something working offline it can work online as well. Conversely, if something works online you should take it offline to double the business!

2. Pick the best experts. A good expert or business owner to partner with should fit the following criteria:

- They're passionate about their topic and are already sharing it with people. An easy way to find out whether an expert has passion, is if they're already naturally inclined to talk about their field of expertise to random people. An expert is very easy to spot at social gatherings, as they somehow always manage to lead a conversation to their topic of interest. A passionate person also tends to share their information and teach it, free of charge. An expert will usually have several people who they've helped *pro bono*.

- They walk their talk. If you find someone who is an expert in health and fitness, they need to be personally fit and healthy. This will make the sales process much easier, as prospects are more likely to buy from someone who is living proof of what they teach.

- They're always researching and learning more. A good expert to partner with is one who attends training or does courses in their field. They'll also subscribe to a few newsletters and membership-based programs. It's important that your experts are ahead of the game in their field to ensure long-term success.

- They love talking to customers and have good people skills. In business, you'll notice there are two types of people. The first type is the person who loves talking with customers and delivering an outstanding customer experience. These people will take to heart any customer complaint and do anything to ensure customers are happy. The second type of person is someone who is more driven by numbers, and loves the thrill of acquiring more and more customers. These people are not particularly attached to providing the ultimate customer experience. Your ideal expert will be the first type. Their commitment to delivering good customer service and experience will ensure the sustainability of the partnership and business.

- They have testimonials or success stories as a result of their expertise. All high-performing webinars include testimonials. Social proof is key when you want to sell on a webinar, so make sure your expert has testimonials. The more positive results and positive outcomes an expert can share as a result of their information, the more sales they're likely to generate. Remember, nothing sells like proof.

- They must be willing to give you fifty per cent of their business. Most experts struggle to sell a $30 product. Therefore, they'll be drawn to someone who is able to provide a platform for them to leverage their knowledge and expertise for a 50-50 share. Fifty per cent of thousands of dollars is more attractive than a hundred per cent of nothing!

- If you currently have a database, make sure their information benefits your audience. If you've spent time and resources building a database of people interested in property investing, your potential partner should have real estate-related expertise or, at least, another investment strategy to leverage your audience. As a facilitator, it will make your job much easier if you can simply plug your experts into your existing database.

3. Approach the experts. An easy way to approach them is by simply looking for them on social media and sending them a message like the one below:

SUBJECT: Webinar Facilitator invitation

Dear Mr. Smith,

My name is **YOUR NAME** and I recently came across your website. I believe I can help you sell a lot more of your products. I specialize in organizing webinars for successful business owners/experts such as you.

Webinars can generate tens of thousands of dollars in sales in just 90 minutes, at no cost to your business. Furthermore, webinars are a great way for you to connect with your audience and increase your sales, authority, and your recognition in your marketplace.

My team and I can set up everything for you.

We do not charge any money for this service, but instead propose a profit-share arrangement. We help you make sales, or we don't get paid a cent.

What we do:

- Set up the live webinar in our system
- Schedule it
- Run the panel and handle questions on the webinar
- Host the webinar if needed, doing intros and outros and calls to action
- Record the live webinar
- Edit and automate the live webinar
- Write and send the email invitations
- Write and send the email follow up for the replay
- Create this automated webinar as a one-page website to catch more leads for your business
- Give you a copy of the webinar to put on your website or blog
- Host the replay for you indefinitely on our hosting system
- Put together your webinar presentation to make sure the webinar converts at 10 per cent minimum, using our powerful and proven sales strategy on webinars
- Help promote the webinar on our social media channels and to our existing contacts

We in turn make a percentage of the sales and are able to use the list again to promote other offers, which may be of interest to the list in the future. If you'd like to discuss this in more detail, please feel free to contact me on **YOUR PHONE NUMBER.**

Warm regards,

YOUR NAME

CASE STUDY: SEAN ALLISON

Initially, when I first met Sean, he purchased my Fast Launch Formula program at $50,000. I helped him put together his first webinar on options trading, and it generated three sales at $997 each with only ten people on his webinar that week. If we'd agreed on an affiliate deal where I'd get fifty per cent of any sales generated from that single webinar, our partnership would have ended making me $1,495.5 in affiliate commissions. He'd have to undertake the responsibility of growing his business by building a list, creating more products and marketing them. Sean wasn't interested in Internet marketing. He only wanted to help his clients and have the best option trading program in the world.

However, at the time, it made more sense for him to give away fifty per cent of his business to me, in exchange for facilitating his webinars. He wouldn't have to worry about the marketing aspect of it.

By implementing the Partnership model, it allowed Sean to have enough time to improve his existing product. It also allowed him to create new products and to focus on providing an excellent customer experience, which was most important to him, and he could also spend the extra time becoming a better options trader. It allowed me, on the other hand, to do what I'm best at and enjoy the most, which is sales and marketing.

This business became a multi-million-dollar business within three years and has been going from strength to strength.

When we created more back-end or high-end profit-maker products it helped take the business to another level. The more experienced you get, the more opportunities you start to see around you. It's like property investing. One person can look at a property and see something that is ready for demolition, while a seasoned investor can see opportunity. A seasoned investor will think that by making a few changes, moving a few things around, adding a few things to the property, they can make a huge return by re-selling it, or revaluing it and taking the newly created equity to invest in another property deal.

Notice I used the words 'newly created'—because rich people know how to create money. My Money-On-Demand system is a way to find experts (like houses) who are undervalued and fix them up (by adding webinars, building the list, adding a high end profit maker product) and converting them into multi-million-dollar businesses that give me at least a 50 per cent return (compared to the standard five to eight per cent return on investment that you can expect from a property). And, unlike houses, they don't have a massive down payment.

I created these businesses from scratch. No money, no capital, just a few hundred dollars for a system like gotowebinar.com. Best of all, the business costs come out of the business before we split 50/50 of the sales revenue.

If I'm going to help a business generate more sales and grow, I want to make money more than once. So look for your own Money-On-Demand partner and start building your own recurring-income-generating assets.

Here's what I love about the Partnership model. I also call this method "The Medical Center model" because it's a similar business model to Medical Centers.

Let me explain.

The Medical Center owner is not a doctor, but he or she makes money from several doctors who pay rent to him. If a doctor stops working, his income stops, but the Medical Center owner just replaces the doctor, so his income isn't affected.

With the partnership model, you have several experts you've helped put together webinars for, who make money from webinars and you get a cut of the sales they make. If they stop working, you just replace one expert with another one.

The image below shows several people that I've helped to create webinars, and the average revenue they make from their webinars every month. I get 50 per cent of each person's business. If one of the businesses falls over, I replace it with another one.

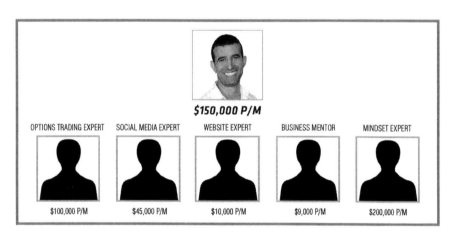

I've had some businesses come and go. For whatever reason they didn't work out, and we just moved on.

Note that I always do everything on a handshake. That may sound scary, but I only work with people who I believe want and need my help. If there's any funny business or anything I don't feel right about I end it early and quickly. I just pack up and move on. I'm happy to say that I've always been paid, because with this Money-On-Demand method, I have total control over the bank accounts, bills, payments and cash flow, and I know I'm going to pay both my business partner and myself on time, every time.

Ask yourself what sort of business you want to run—the sort where you control the money and remain behind-the-scenes, or the sort where you work with customers and create products without having to worry about management and logistics? There's nothing wrong with either one, but note that you can't do both well. If you're good at one aspect of the business, you need someone else to handle the other.

CHAPTER 5

WEBINAR FACILITATION

Unlike the previous chapter where you own a share of the webinar business (you create a company with the webinar owner and you own a 50 per cent share of the company) the Webinar Facilitation model is a one-off transaction. You get a cut of the profit only from the webinar you help to set up.

In fact, all my Partnerships start out first with the Webinar Facilitation method. When I identify a potential partner, I start by running a webinar where I receive 50 per cent one-off commissions of the sales generated from that single webinar. I gauge how they do business, how they sell, how they listen to me (or not) on feedback, and how good their customer service and follow up process is. I find out if they care about results or just money. I use this as a test to see whether we can do business together on another, more long-term level. Some of these people become partners and most don't. We just make money together once or a few times a year. I'm not looking to partner with everyone, just the amazing ones—the unique ones—where I can see I can contribute and there can be a big win/win/win. This means a win for the customers, a win for the expert and a win for me. If there isn't a win/win/win situation, the business won't last. If the expert doesn't make enough money they'll get annoyed and leave. If the customers don't get results the business can't grow and gets a bad name, and if I don't make money it's not worth my time.

The Webinar Facilitation strategy is the simple process of finding an expert with a lot of knowledge and experience about a topic, and a good-size following, and helping them put together and launch a webinar. This can bring thousands of dollars in net profit.

The difference between the Partnership strategy and the Webinar Facilitation strategy, is that with the Partnership model, you own a share of the webinar business. In other words, you create a company with the webinar owner and you own a fifty per cent share of the company.

The Webinar Facilitation method is much simpler. It is a one-off transaction. You only get a cut of the profit from the webinar you helped set up.

The only skills needed by a facilitator are:

- Knowing how to structure a webinar (introduction, content and close)
- Understanding what makes a good webinar
- Knowing how to schedule a live webinar
- Knowing how to send an email invitation
- Knowing how to create an offer and price it

Webinar Facilitation — Creating multiple streams of income

1. Find an expert.
   As the whole facilitation process only takes a few hours, finding experts who have an audience but are yet to leverage the power of webinars should become your priority.

I recommend that you approach authors, speakers, coaches, and experts—professionals who are too busy in their business or practice and facilitate webinars for them.

These people usually have a lot of knowledge to share, have authority status and usually have case studies of success stories. They have an audience and are usually on the brink of burnout and are looking for leverage. So it's an easy decision for them when you offer them the opportunity to automate their sales process and product delivery at no upfront cost.

The best way to find and approach these people is by looking at recent books on amazon.com, or by performing a Google search, and then contacting them through their website or social media.

2. Structure the webinar.
   This is relatively easy. Provided a webinar is 60 minutes, the first 10 minutes should include:

   - The headline (the title of the webinar). This should be enticing, to arouse the audience's curiosity and compel them to register.

   - The answer to the question, "what led me to this webinar?" Explain to the audience why the presenter is in a position to share their information and what makes them an authority on the subject.

   - Case studies or testimonials. To emphasize the expert status of the presenter, it's important to introduce case studies or testimonials. These are stories about people who have implemented what is about to be shared, and as a result have experienced a positive outcome.

3. Rehearse
    The expert should rehearse the presentation several times by going through the slides as if talking to a live audience. Ideally, this should be in front of you, the facilitator, so that you can ensure that the webinar is of the highest quality.

Over the years, I've assessed thousands of webinars using the checklist below:

> Big Benefit: *Did the presenter give you the desire to stay on the webinar by stating the big benefit of listening to him at the start?*
>
> Their Story: *Was their story credible? Did the presenter gain your trust, respect and interest?*
>
> Proof: *Was there proof to back up their claims?*
>
> Testimonials: *Were they realistic and short? Did the clients avoid reading them word for word?*
>
> Statistics: *Did they quote the source of the statistics they mentioned? Were there too many statistics or too few? Were they relevant?*
>
> Images: *Did they use pictures to illustrate the points made? Were the pictures relevant?*
>
> Length of intro: *Did it exceed ten minutes?*

Steps: *Did they break down their presentation into easy-to-follow steps? Did they state the benefits of following each step?*

Content: *Did they deliver their content one bullet point at a time?*

Stories: *Did the presenter tell stories to back up their points/steps?*

Case studies: *Were there case studies to support their content?*

Information: *Were there good, valuable tips shared?*

Interaction: *Did they ask questions to engage the audience?*

Transition: *Did the presenter transition into the close smoothly?*

Product: *Did the presenter use one whole slide to display the product?*

Benefits vs. Features: *Did the presenter focus on talking about the features of the product 30 per cent of the time and focus on talking about the benefits of the product 70 per cent of the time?*

Value: *Did the presenter underline the value of each item included in the product?*

Bonuses: *Were the free bonuses of high perceived value?*

Guarantee: *Was there a risk reversal guarantee such as a money-back guarantee?*

Clear offer: *Was just one clear offer made or was the offer confusing?*

Call to action: *Was this on time and clear? Was it announced with confidence?*

4. Schedule the webinar.
   When scheduling live webinars with platforms such as gotowebinar.com, it only takes three to five minutes.

   The information that you need to enter is:

   - The title of the webinar
   - Its description
   - The time and date of the broadcast
   - The time zone

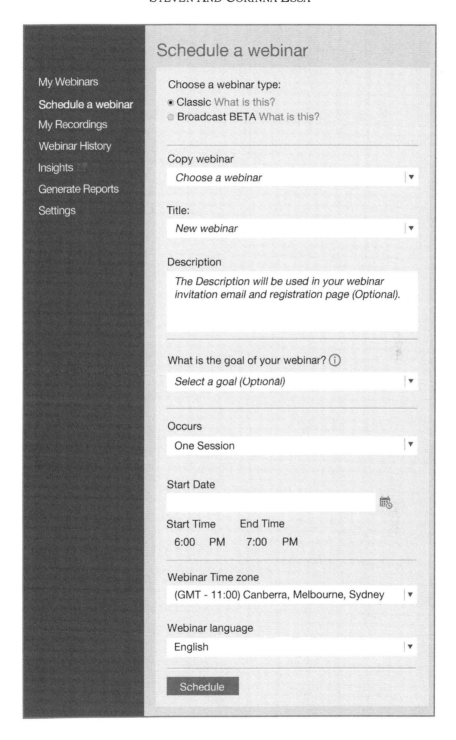

Once the webinar has been scheduled, web conferencing services such as gotowebinar.com will give you the registration link to share with potential registrants, which looks like this: https://attendee.gotowebinar.com/register/3876772 815202280450

5. Shorten the link.
   If you want to turn this registration link into a prettier, shorter link, it can easily be done using domain forwarding or domain masking services such as bitly.com.

6. Write the email invitation.
   When writing the email invitation to a live webinar, it's important to have an attention-grabbing subject line. Remember, people are inundated with emails every day, so consider what will make your email stand out from all the noise.

   When writing an email to entice people to click on a link, it's important to make sure that the copy sells the *link* rather than the *product* (in this case the webinar). Writing copy that points to the link rather than the product/webinar will result in higher click-through rates—the proportion of people who click on the registration link—and therefore will increase the webinar registration rate.

   The email should be short and have an appealing start, to entice people to keep reading. It should also include the call to action three times, spread across the email, and a 'p.s.' that acts as a summary of the main benefit of registering, including a sense of urgency.

Below is a webinar registration email template that has worked very well for us in a wide range of niches:

SUBJECT: Grab your 5-Step Proven social media monetization system [TRAINING]

Hello (firstname)

Before you market your business on social media again, make sure you watch this training first, titled:

The Proven 5-Step Social Media Monetization System Revealed

Wednesday, December 21st

****

11am AEDT (Sydney time)
REGISTRATION LINK

OR

8pm AEDT (Sydney time) / 9am GMT (London time)
REGISTRATION LINK

****

During this 1-hour LIVE training, world-renowned social media strategist *Corinna Essa* will reveal:

- How to effectively **market your business on social media in under an hour a day**
- The 3 ways to **build a big, targeted and engaged audience** on social media
- The little-known social media marketing hack that is **10 times more effective than print ads**
- **What the smartest brands are doing on social media** right now and how to copy their success formula

---

- How to **place your ads on any website** for free
- How to **build an email list of 1,000 people in 30 days** so you <u>never have to worry about traffic again</u>

And much, much more!

* *

11am AEDT (Sydney time)
<u>REGISTRATION LINK</u>

OR

8pm AEDT (Sydney time) / 9am GMT (London time)
<u>REGISTRATION LINK</u>

* *

Don't miss this opportunity to finally discover what works and what doesn't.

Enjoy!

SIGNATURE

PS. This training won't run again in the near future so make sure you secure your place.

* *

11am AEDT (Sydney time)
<u>REGISTRATION LINK</u>

OR

8pm AEDT (Sydney time) / 9am GMT (London time)
<u>REGISTRATION LINK</u>

* *

7. Bonus tip: Facilitate replays for ten times the profit

As a facilitator, your job doesn't have to end at sending out an email. By recording the live webinar and automating it using software such as webinator.biz, you could just as easily create a new passive, recurring income stream from the commissions generated from the replay you set up.

You email the replay to all registrants. Those who attended may wish to watch it again or share it with their contacts. Those who registered but did not attend may wish to watch it for the first time.

Gotowebinar.com allows you to send emails within its platform to all registrants, and segments them according to those who attended and those who didn't attend:

Emails

Reply-to: Steven and Corinna Essa, webinars@x10effect.com

Confirmation Email to Registrants: Send upon registration	Edit
No reminder email to Attendees, Co-organizers and Panelists	
Follow-up Email to Attendees: Send 1 Day after the session	Edit
No follow-up email to Absentees.	Edit

CASE STUDY: DOMINIQUE GRUBISA

Back in 2009, Dominique, a barrister, was in a very interesting position. She specialized in helping people get out of debt, a service that usually costs around $15,000.

This was a great niche, especially at the time of the financial crisis with so many people going broke and bank foreclosures at record highs. With many lending bodies lending too much to people who didn't qualify, debt-busting barrister Dominique Grubisa had the opportunity to make a real difference for these people. She'd nearly gone bankrupt herself. The banks and lawyers tried to take her down and she had learned quickly how to address and reverse her situation.

She'd put together a unique method to help people avoid filing for bankruptcy, and created software that automated the process of writing hardship letters to banks. She shared with me that she was about to appear on *A Current Affair* (a popular mainstream TV show that covers news and current affairs). Since they were about to interview Dominique, it was a great opportunity for her to build a large following.

In the show, Dominique was invited to help an everyday Australian family that was caught up in the financial crisis by investing in many homes. The father was going bankrupt, and Dominique's job was to show him and the viewers at home how to reduce his $30,000 a month in negative cash flow to $600. It was a real life case study.

NOTE: If you or your expert can prove what you do live, do it! There is nothing more powerful than demonstrating something in real time. On a live webinar, or during a live talk, these demonstrations—also known as 'dramatic demonstrations'—are extremely effective. This is why you'll see many presenters take a person from the audience and prove in front of everyone else that what they do works. This will increase your sales conversion considerably as most people watching will say internally, "I want him/her to do that for me." When putting together webinars, whether for yourself or for someone else, always ask yourself how you can include a dramatic demonstration.

When I first helped Sean Allison (ex-government employee from Perth) put together his webinar on options trading, I soon realized that including a dramatic demonstration would help improve his conversions. Now, in the middle of his presentation, Sean logs in to his trading account and places trades to show people both how easy it is and the income potential.

In the case of Dominique Grubisa, the TV producer didn't allow her to advertise her services during her guest appearance, but allowed her to host a live chat on the *A Current Affair* website. Not surprisingly, the people watching at home who were in similar or worse trouble than the family on the show wanted to talk to her. They rushed to their computers to chat to her online.

Since this was a fantastic opportunity for her to build a database of prospects, I created a lead-capture form to collect their names and emails, which she mentioned during the live chat.

A lead-capture form is simply a box that is usually placed at the top right hand side of a web page, which allows people to submit their contact details (such as their name and email address) in exchange for a free offer or newsletter subscription.

In Dominique's case, her lead-capture form offered a piece of software, automating the process of writing hardship letters. This alone resulted in building a mailing list of over 1,000, hot, hungry prospects in 24 hours. She later told me that the number ended up at well over 3,000 people.

The next step was to nurture these prospects with quality, relevant information and offer products and services. At first, Dominique wanted to travel around the country and deliver local seminars, which could end up costing thousands of dollars, with no guarantee of attendance or return on investment. I advised her to deliver a webinar instead. The choice was obvious to me. Spend money on flights, accommodation, hotels, food and marketing—or set up a webinar and talk to these people from home for free? Which would you rather do?

Initially, she didn't agree with me. However, I persisted and finally convinced her. I argued that we could help these people this week instead of in six week's time when most would already be bankrupt or homeless.

This was a really tough time for many people and many were scared for their families and future. The sooner we shared Dominique's knowledge, the better. Most couldn't afford to wait for a solution any longer and neither could

Dominique if she hoped to turn her knowledge into a real business. The clock was ticking.

Since Dominique had a lot of knowledge and experience when it came to debt rescue, as well as testimonials, case studies and the ability to state, 'as seen on TV', she had all the ingredients for putting together a successful webinar.

However, she was stuck when it came to putting together an offer, and pricing the offer. This is a common situation with experts who trade their time for money. They don't know how to productize their knowledge or expertise.

I asked her the following simple question, which helped her to come up with a product idea:
"At the end of the free webinar, Dominique, how can you help people further?" Ask any expert how they can further help people and they'll give you the answers.

Dominique started to list what she could do if they wanted more one-on-one help from her. The list included:

- Teaching them how to acquire good assets and put them in a trust
- Helping them write hardship letters to creditors to negotiate interest rates
- Weekly webinars to coach people going through financial hardship

NOTE: What I try to do with an expert that doesn't already have a product or hasn't sold something before, is to offer things that we don't have to create if nobody buys them. For example, I wouldn't tell Dominique to offer a book she hadn't written yet because a book could take months to write and what if only one person bought it? She would still need to write it. Instead, I like to create an offer that consists of things we can deliver *after* people buy.

I explain that we're only going to do this once. We're testing the market—and if the webinar converts and we generate sales, then we can find a way to automate the process after the first webinar. The first and most important element we need to ensure is whether or not the webinar converts into sales. Without a sale we have no business, so why waste time creating something if it doesn't sell?

Once we created an outline of her product, I asked Dominique how much she could charge for it. As she was unsure, my next question was, "How much would another lawyer charge to deliver what we just outlined?" To my surprise, she answered $15,000. So, when it came to pricing her product, anything lower than $15,000 would still give her a competitive advantage.

Since Dominique was able to hire her mother, a retired solicitor, to help her deliver the product, and use her software to speed up the process of writing hardship letters, she was happy to charge as little as $3,000. This was a fifth of the going rate, which made her product an irresistible offer—and that's what you should put together. Not good offers, not bargains, but irresistible offers. As the old cliché says: "make them an offer they can't refuse."

Once the webinar was put together, I scheduled the live webinar using gotowebinar.com and I emailed the list generated from her television appearance, inviting them to register for it.

The webinar generated six sales at $3,000 each, a total of $18,000.

She went on to make over $100,000 in six months from that list alone. She has now generated millions of dollars from that same webinar presentation. She now charges $5500 for that product (with some add–ons) but essentially, her current product is the one I helped her put together in just a few hours. A product that has helped many people and made her a multi-millionaire—just another in the long list of millionaires my Webinar Facilitation system has helped to create.

CHAPTER 6

AFFILIATE STRATEGY

Affiliate marketing is the process of promoting other people's products on the Internet for a commission.

There are many affiliate networks available, such as clickbank.com, which list thousands of products in various different niches, for which anyone can become an affiliate. Commissions range from fifty per cent to seventy-five per cent, and all affiliates are free to join.

Standard affiliate marketing usually consists of signing up as an affiliate for a particular product and sending traffic to the affiliate link using email marketing, blogging, social networks and other forms of traffic.

However, when it comes to these standard affiliate marketing strategies, you can miss a lot of sales opportunities.

Let me explain.

When an affiliate puts effort into sending traffic to an affiliate product, the majority of visitors choose to opt-in to the free offer first. (Most websites selling a product include the option for people to submit their contact details in exchange for a free offer.) This means that the product owner is generating leads that can be used for marketing for years to come, from the effort of the affiliate.

The affiliate, on the other hand, has to generate traffic for a chance to make a sale—and is not capturing any leads. Considering that a standard website converts at one per cent, the affiliate would have to drive 100 visitors to a web page for a sale to occur, and would need to drive traffic to a web page constantly in order to make substantial income from it.

However, when combining affiliate marketing with the power of webinars, you not only benefit from a ten per cent conversion rate (as webinars usually convert at ten per cent), you capture the leads before the product owner does.

In addition, should you choose to sell an affiliate product on a webinar, which is priced below the preferred price point of minimum $297, it is easy to add value to the product by adding other services and products for yourself.

For example, should you be selling a $97 course as an affiliate, when adding a few one-to-one coaching sessions, adding a done-for-you service, a ready-made template, an interview recording, etc.... the whole bundle could easily be sold for more.

Therefore, the Money-On-Demand affiliate strategy is a more lucrative business model than the standard affiliate marketing strategy, allowing you to sell ten times more products, at a higher price point, while simultaneously building your list, for the same amount of effort.

Affiliate — No product? No problem

1. When using the Affiliate strategy, the process is exactly the same as with any webinar. Firstly, you devise an attention-grabbing headline,

2. Write an introduction,
3. Break the content into easy-to-follow steps,
4. Write a pitch,
5. Point people to your affiliate link in order to purchase the product

An affiliate link is usually a long, quite ugly URL, which can easily be masked using a WordPress plugin such as 'pretty link'.

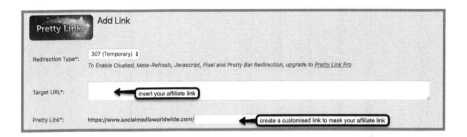

The plugin will allow you to use a domain name of your choice that you've purchased, and use it to mask the long affiliate link. Therefore, you end up sending people to a link that looks like www.yourdomainname.com/special instead.

CASE STUDY: HOW I CAME UP WITH THE MONEY-ON-DEMAND AFFILIATE STRATEGY

I often wondered what would be the best way to prove to people that webinars are the best cash flow generating strategy on the web, bar none.

I came up with the idea that I could put together and launch a webinar from scratch for someone, in front of a live audience. All I'd need was a willing person, an Internet connection and access to a computer.

When I shared the idea with my wife Corinna, her eyes immediately lit up. What a great idea to prove in front of a live audience how webinars are the fastest and easiest way to make money online! It became a major priority on our to-do list.

I was on vacation with Mark Anastasi, who had just released his New York Times best selling book, *The Laptop Millionaire*. In between boating, spear fishing, snorkeling and relaxing on the beach, I suggested that Mark should go on tour to promote his book. His book covers over 21 ways to make money online, and includes our webinar strategies.

Mark loved the idea of a world tour to deliver seminars on online wealth creation, and we agreed to use that opportunity to showcase the power of webinars in front of a live audience.

The three-day seminar tour, *The Laptop Millionaire World Tour*, went to twelve cities around the world. In every city, hundreds of people gathered, and on the first day of the seminar, the attendees willing to participate in the challenge would come up on stage and have a few seconds to pitch their webinar idea to the rest of the audience.

The remaining attendees who were not participating then voted for the best idea through clapping. The first three-day seminar took place in Melbourne, where Shane Price, a business consultant, was voted by the audience to present his webinar.

His webinar ended up generating $21,425 in under 90 minutes. Later, more sales came in boosting the total revenue to over $35,000.

We knew we were onto something. The challenge became very popular as people found out about our seminars—how some people were leaving our seminars thousands of dollars richer. Soon, we'd have more challenge contestants on stage than voters in the audience.

The first selection criteria was for the person to have a webinar idea, but had never used webinars to monetize their idea. The finalist was decided by audience applause.

Once the challenge winner was selected, he or she had to spend the rest of the day filling in my one-million-dollar-webinar-formula template—with slides—which has been responsible for generating over 50 million dollars in sales for my clients and me. The template includes:

- The headline (the webinar title)
- The introduction, explaining what led the presenter to deliver this presentation
- The content (which teaches the strategy)
- The close (which presents the product offer and call to action). Note that in all cases, the product hadn't been created yet.

Wait a minute, the product wasn't created yet?

That's right, we *never* create the product until we've sold it, and customers actually prefer it that way. More on that later in this book.

Once the challenge winner had finished putting together the slides, they were sent to my graphic designers for branding.

On the second day, while the seminar was being delivered, the contestant had to use that time to practice the webinar, making sure that it flowed well, wasn't too thin in terms of content, and didn't go overtime. We'd then schedule the live webinar on gotowebinar.com to be delivered at 11am on the final day. Once the webinar was scheduled, an email to our database would be sent out, inviting people to watch the live presentation.

Unlike other webinars, where we'd allow three days to promote it, we had just one shot at getting enough attendees to generate sales. At 11am the next day, the contestant stood on the stage and delivered the live webinar while attendees watched the process.

The process enabled random attendees, some of whom had never generated any money online, to make from $2,000 to $22,000 in as little as 90 minutes.
We'd proved our point.

In Sydney, however, an interesting thing happened which led us to discover a brand new way to leverage webinars ... even without having to put together a product or deliver a product ...

The lucky Sydney contestant, Helen, won the challenge with the idea, *How to make a million dollars thanks to Pinterest.*

At the time, Pinterest was a new social network that was proving to be a very promising platform in terms of traffic, leads and sales generation.

When Helen was then asked to put together the webinar slides, she confessed she'd no desire to put together a Pinterest-related information course to sell at the end of the webinar. I wish I'd known that earlier! It's always best if the experts you work with have a passion for delivering information and helping people.

When I put the PowerPoint slides together for Helen's webinar, everything was going fine. However, when I asked her what she wanted to offer— coaching, a done-for-you service, one-on-one consultations, a one-day workshop, or more webinars to teach them how to use Pinterest she replied: NONE! NONE? I was shocked! "How are you going to help these people then?" I asked. She said she wasn't interested in doing more work after the webinar—she thought it would just be cool to do a webinar, share her knowledge, and that's it.

Usually, if a winner was picked by the audience, I asked: Do you want to work with customers? Do you love customer service? If they said no, I said next. But in Sydney we had only a few hours to put together a webinar and present it live. The clock was ticking.... Time was running out and I had to do something.

Although we'd been taking contestants through the process of putting together a free webinar to sell a course or product and then delivering the product or course after it was sold, in Helen's case I had to think fast about an alternative.

The easiest way for Helen to have a course to sell, was to become an affiliate of someone else's product. I searched on

Google for the best and latest Pinterest course, which led us to finding a product that had an affiliate program and was priced at $97.

Although $97 is usually too low a price point for a product to sell on a webinar, as we often recommend people to sell products on webinars for $297 or more, in Helen's case she wouldn't have to do anything after the webinar. All she had to do, was point the webinar attendees who wanted to learn more about Pinterest, to buy the course through her affiliate link.

For every sale that went through her affiliate link, she received a fifty per cent commission. Best of all, she didn't have to handle any customer support enquiries, or any customer related questions. The product owner was handling everything.

What was great about this example is that the product was already created, so when people purchased it they could instantly get access to it. We used pictures of the product images on the product owner's website in Helen's PowerPoint, which made it look even better and there was no issue from the audience when Helen transitioned into selling someone else's product. She positioned the expert as the authority and best at Pinterest at that time and it had no effect on the sales. This, once more, proves my theory that you can't say the wrong thing to the right audience. "Don't sweat the small stuff." As they say. Don't worry about the little details that stop most people starting their business ... just do it.

Helen's webinar, which generated over $2,200 in sales, proved once again that webinars are the fastest and easiest way to make money online ... regardless of whether you even have a product to sell or not!

CHAPTER 7

PAID WEBINAR

People buy tickets to attend conferences and seminars, and more and more these days, people buy tickets to attend live webinars. The benefits are that there are no travel costs involved for the attendees, and no exorbitant conference room hire costs for the organizer. An added benefit is that people can attend the webinar regardless of their geographic location. This makes the process of selling webinar seats much easier for the organizer, because it removes an important sale objection.

To ensure a smooth delivery, you need a decent Internet connection (from 2 to 5 megabits a second in terms of download speed and 0.85 megabits a second in terms of upload speed) for the organizer. A useful tool for checking a computer's upload and download speed is speedtest.net.

To set up a paid webinar, the following is required:

- A quality, content-rich webinar presentation
- An online payment processing facility
- Traffic from a targeted audience (in the form of an email list or social media following)

Paid Webinar — The art of getting paid upfront

1. Make sure you have a top-of-the-range webinar

When planning to sell a webinar, the information shared must be of the highest quality bar none. This is because, when the webinar is over, your audience must feel that they have got their money's worth. The length of the webinar doesn't necessarily matter, since people are after quality rather than quantity, but the information shared is of the highest importance. Information that is common knowledge, or can be found easily elsewhere won't be as appealing as ground-breaking and eye-opening information.

Therefore, focusing on sharing high quality content when it comes to pre-paid webinars is of the highest importance. Audience members should have at least four or five 'aha' moments. They must leave the webinar feeling that they now have an advantage over someone who did not attend the webinar.

Paid webinars should share information such as:

- What is about to happen (attendees value insights into the future)
- Resources (where to find further information about the topics shared)
- Access to templates and free downloads
- Case studies
- Question and answer session

When it comes to paid webinars, the same format as free webinars can be used:

- Introduction (answering: who am I? why am I sharing this information with you? and, what qualifies me to share this information?)
- Content (structured in three, five or seven steps, making it easier for attendees to assimilate the information)

- Close (either offering further paid products or services, free resources, or instructions on how to get in contact with the presenter for further information)
- Question and answer session

2. Organize an online payment facility for ticket sales. Anyone today can process sales online using payment facilities such as paypal.com. Creating a "payment link" only takes a few steps, as shown below:

PayPal will allow you to create a payment link. When buyers click on it, it will redirect them to a payment page. PayPal also provides the html code of the link so it can be embedded on any web page as a "buy" button:

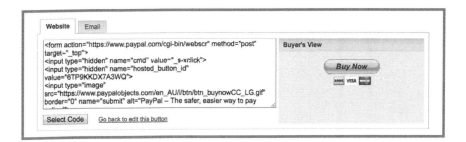

The main disadvantage of using PayPal is their high processing fees.

Alternatively, if you already have an online merchant facility, software tools such as infusionsoft.com and 1shoppingcart.com allow you to create secure payment pages which link to your merchant account—like the one below:

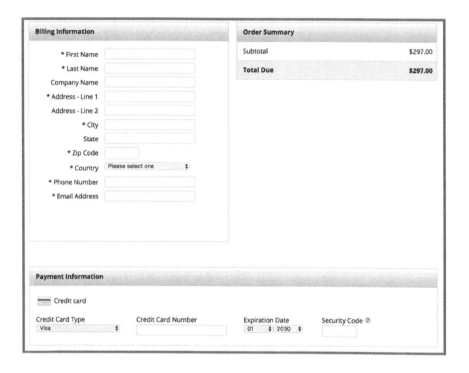

Once buyers submit their payment information, the money collected goes straight to your bank account.

3. Provide the buyer with the webinar access details.
   You can set this up by creating an automatic follow-up email to buyers, using systems such as infusionsoft.com, 1shoppingcart.com or paypal.com. When the buyers have completed their payment, they

automatically receive a confirmation email together with access details such as the one below:

Dear Steve,

Thank you for registering for "The 5-Step Proven Social Media Monetization System Revealed 11am AEDT".

In this webinar you'll discover:

• How to effectively market your business on social media in under an hour a day
• The 4 ways to monetize your social media right now, even if you don't have a product or business
• The 3 ways to build a big, targeted and engaged audience on social media
• The little-known social media marketing hack that is 10 times more effective than print ads
• How to place your ads on any website for free
• How to build an email list fast so you never have to worry about traffic again

And much, much more!

Please send your questions, comments and feedback to: webinars@x10effect.com

How To Join The Webinar

Wed, Dec 21, 2016 11:00 AM - 12:30 PM AEDT

Add to Calendar: Outlook® Calendar | Google Calendar&#8482 | iCal®

1. **Click the link to join the webinar at the specified time and date:**

   https://global.gotowebinar.com/join/1993424855828952833/855112258

   Before joining, be sure to check system requirements to avoid any connection issues.
   Note: This link should not be shared with others; it is unique to you.

2. **Choose one of the following audio options:**
   TO USE YOUR COMPUTER'S AUDIO:
   When the webinar begins, you will be connected to audio using your computer's microphone and speakers (VoIP). A headset is recommended.
   --OR--
   TO USE YOUR TELEPHONE:
   If you prefer to use your phone, you must select "Use Telephone" after joining the webinar and call in using the numbers below.
   Australia: +61 3 8488 8990
   Access Code: 234-834-556
   Audio PIN: Shown after joining the webinar
   Calling from another country?

---

4. Sell tickets to the pre-paid webinar.

There are many traffic strategies that you can use:

- **Your mailing list**
  If you already own a list of people likely to be interested in your pre-paid webinar, send an

average of three emails in the space of a week prior to the webinar. This should get you a considerable number of sales, depending on the list size and quality.

- **Joint Ventures**
  If you know people with mailing lists that contain your target market, this can represent considerable leverage. Secure a joint venture with them, where they promote your pre-paid webinar in exchange for a flat fee, sales commission, or a reciprocal mailing. This could also bring many sales depending on the list size and quality.

- **Solo ads**
  Solo ads involve paying a flat fee to a list owner, to email their list on your behalf. Solo ad providers can be found in places such as udimi.com. These provide a guaranteed number of clicks, so you can rest assured you get the traffic you paid for. Solo ads can produce very good results at a reasonable price.

- **Social media**
  Generating traffic from social networks such as Facebook, Twitter or LinkedIn can be highly effective, regardless of your audience size. What makes these channels effective is the fact that your existing contacts can easily share your post promoting your pre-paid webinar. When you consider that each social media user has an average of 140 contacts, tapping into people's audiences for free has never been faster and easier.

When preparing the marketing material, the same principles used with free webinars apply. Advertise a minimum of four days prior to the event. This will ensure the maximum amount of sales. And make sure the promotional material such as email copy includes the following:

- A big promise which arouses interest and curiosity (to entice people to read through most of the promotional copy)
- Bullet points (a list of benefits that will be covered during the webinar)
- Two to three calls to action throughout the copy (every sentence or paragraph should point to the call to action)
- Scarcity (reminding people of how time sensitive the offer is)
- Bonuses (optional) to entice people and reward them for taking action

Timing can play a major role in the success of a webinar and especially a pre-paid webinar. When the topic covered is 'timely' and close to breaking news, it can seriously impact the amount of sales generated.

Carefully scripting the invitation to a pre-paid webinar is as important as the webinar itself. Unlike free webinars where you have 90 minutes to get people to know you, like you, trust you, and therefore buy from you, the success of paid webinars is heavily reliant on the marketing and copy used.

An added benefit of a pre-paid live webinar, is the ability to turn the recording into a stand-alone product for evergreen profits—more of that in the next chapter.

CASE STUDY: HARRY DENT

When I was speaking at a conference in Sydney, I bumped into a seminar promoter who worked closely with economist Harry Dent.

Harry Dent is an economist who reviews the economy in the US—and the world—and forecasts market peaks, crashes and global trends.

At the time of the meeting, the media was focused on news about the Chinese stock market crash, which was very much aligned with Harry Dent's recent forecasts about the Chinese economy.

People were increasingly concerned about the future of their investments, so this was a good opportunity to deliver a webinar about the topic.

Harry and I put together a pre-paid 90 minute-long webinar for investors, titled, *The China Tsunami: The Next Global Crash Is Happening,* for $97.

In the webinar, Harry Dent would cover the reasons behind China's stock market crash, the impact it would have on other countries and tips on how to protect your investments.

The invitation was sent three times during a three-day period, to a list of a few thousand people who had in the past expressed interest in wealth creation and investment education. The following invitation was sent:

REVEALED: HARRY DENT'S DIRE WARNING AND HIS STRATEGY TO AVOID IMMINENT DISASTER IN THIS NOT-TO-BE MISSED 90 MINUTE **LIVE** WEBINAR

Hear When and Why the Smart Money Left China—and Learn How This Fact Created this Week's Global Crash

- What Do China's Captains of Industry Know about the Failing Chinese Economy that YOU don't?
- Why Have The Richest 1 per cent in China Moved their Wealth From China and Invested In Overseas Real Estate Markets Like Brisbane and Sydney (at Over-Inflated Prices)?
- What Will Happen In The Next Days, Weeks And Months?
- What Can You Do NOW To Protect Yourself?

Learn Why Every Asset Class in The World has destabilized—Where Are the Safe Havens?

- How Can YOU Protect Yourself from the Inevitable Global Crash of Stocks and Real Estate that Will Follow China's Demise?
- What Are The 'Smart Money' Investors Doing Right Now To Secure their Wealth?
- Can You Avoid Making The Popular 'Dumb Money Investments' that Seem Safe, but are Simply Pouring Good Money into Bad, Overvalued, Risky Assets?

Will Your Investment Portfolios in The Share Market and Real Estate Get Decimated If You Do Nothing?

In this content packed 90-minute webinar, Leading Global Economist, Harry S. Dent will cover the following:

1. China's inevitable destination!
2. What will happen to the world?
3. How low will gold go?
4. The brand new prediction on oil over the coming months and why!
5. What will happen to the Aussie dollar?
6. Can the Dow Jones and NASDAQ dodge the Bullet?

When: 11am AEST, Friday August 28th

Cost: $97.00 AUD

Availability: only 100 webinar seats available—THIS WILL SELL OUT!!!

(Note: Once you've paid via Visa, AMEX, MasterCard or PayPal via the 'Buy Now' button below, you'll be sent an email from GOKO Management to continue to the Harry Dent webinar.)

This led to over 160 sales at $97, which is $15,520 in total—not bad for 90 minutes!

There are many reasons why this pre-paid webinar converted well.

- It was timely. China's market crash was a hot topic all over the media, and was a threat to many investors around the world.

- A lot of eyes were on Harry Dent, since only a year prior to the crash, he'd predicted the Chinese declining economy. A large number of people were showing interest in what was about to happen next.

- The enticing headline (webinar title) which arouses both curiosity and interest.

- More than ten bullet points were used, making it easy for people to read through the promotional material while emphasizing the benefits of attending the webinar.

- The genuine urgency and scarcity elements of the webinar. The webinar platform being used was gotowebinar.com, which had a limit of 100 live attendees. That meant that people who didn't secure their place in time would miss the opportunity not only to participate in the LIVE broadcast, but also the opportunity of ever watching the event. There was no mention of a replay in the invitation. The added warning that the webinar 'will sell out' not only made more people eager to secure their place, it also made them act immediately.

CHAPTER 8

INCOME LOOPS

Webinars can bring a significant amount of money upfront (as much as $200,000 in 90 minutes has been reported). However, webinars can also generate significant recurring revenue.

The Money-On-Demand Loop strategy is the process of storing your webinar recordings on a membership site and charging a monthly fee for access to them. This allows you to generate recurring revenue without having to exchange time for money.

What is required:

- A WordPress site
- Hosting
- The 'Wishlist' WordPress plugin

Together, these allow you to store unlimited videos, webinars and documents in a password-protected area on the web.

Loop Strategy — Generating autopilot income

1. Install the Wishlist plugin on your website.
   The Wishlist plugin is easy to use and manage. It allows you to have unlimited membership levels, should you wish to provide different types of access for different customers.

For example, you can easily have three types of memberships like the ones below:

- Standard ($47 a month)
- Gold ($67 a month)
- Platinum ($97 a month)

The subscription management aspect is also very user-friendly. Not only can you move members from one level to another very easily, should they wish to upgrade or downgrade, you can also just as easily stop access for members who have cancelled their subscription.

In addition, the upgrade process is completely automated, because when members try to access content not included in their membership level, they get the message below:

Oops! Wrong Membership Level

....

If you have been redirected to this page it means your membership level does not include the feature you selected. To take advantage of other features on this site see table below on what is included with each membership level.

---

2. Put together the content for the membership site
   When putting this content together, structure is very important.

   Content in a membership site should never be uncategorized, random information, scattered across the site. Your site should take your members through specific steps in a logical order. That way they feel like they're making progress.

   You should map out the content so that members are taken from point A (not knowing anything about the topic) to point B (having mastered the skill they were taught).

   For example, let's assume you wish to educate members on how to set up and run an eBook business and wish your members to stay subscribed for a minimum of six months. You could potentially structure your content in this way:

   - PHASE 1: Market research
   - PHASE 2: Writing your eBook
   - PHASE 3: Paid traffic generation
   - PHASE 4: Free traffic generation
   - PHASE 5: Automation
   - PHASE 6: Upsells

Each phase would then be broken into weeks (four weeks per phase). Each week could consist of one webinar, which is also broken down in steps as shown here:

- Webinar 1: Title
- Step 1
- Step 2
- Step 3
- Homework
- Resources
- Accompanying documents

Therefore, based on the eBook example above, PHASE 1 could include the following 4 webinars:

PHASE 1: Market research

Webinar 1 (week 1): How to come up with eBook ideas
- Step 1: Check the latest best selling eBooks on Amazon.com
- Step 2: Read Amazon reviews to find out what people are looking for
- Step 3: Compile a list of best potential eBook topics
  o Homework: List the 10 best selling books on Amazon.com and include the most insightful reviews for each and highlight the eBook topics with the most potential
  o Resources: Amazon research tool
  o Accompanying documents: .pdf on how to perform research effectively on Amazon

Webinar 2 (week 2): How to research eBook topics on Youtube.com
- Step 1: Watch the most viewed YouTube videos about your best potential eBook topics
- Step 2: Read the comments left for each video on Youtube.com
- Step 3: List the most common tips revealed on the most viewed YouTube videos
  - Homework: Implement all 3 steps
  - Resources: YouTube research tool
  - Accompanying documents: .pdf on how to perform research effectively on Youtube.com

Webinar 3 (week 3): How to research eBook topics on print publications
- Step 1: Identify the most popular magazines around the best eBook topics
- Step 2: Check the front cover and look at headlines
- Step 3: Find out the circulation of each magazine (to identify potential reach)
  - Homework: List the five most popular magazines around the best eBook topics and find out their circulation
  - Resources: Rolodex of most popular magazines
  - Accompanying documents: .pdf with the website addresses of the most popular magazines

Webinar 4 (week 4): How to perform keyword research
- Step 1: Choose a keyword research tool
- Step 2: Start your keyword research

- Step 3: Identify the most highly searched keywords
  - o Homework: perform keyword research on your potential eBook topics and list them in order of importance on a spreadsheet
  - o Resources: a keyword research tool
  - o Accompanying documents: .pdf on how to use the keyword research tool

By structuring your content this way, members are more likely to get faster results, and therefore remain loyal. In addition, having milestones increases the likelihood of members staying subscribed for the whole cycle.

Because people learn in different ways, including the same content in different formats can also set your membership site apart from others. For example, you can offer your content in .pdf format by simply transcribing your webinars, or in mp3 format, which allows people to listen to content while on the move.

Adding homework at the end of each lesson (webinar) also offers the opportunity to members to take action, remain engaged and assimilate the information. They implement each strategy and remain committed to the subscription.

Including a resource document, a frequently asked questions document and templates and checklists to accompany each webinar will also set your membership site apart.

3. Promote your membership site.

The best way to cultivate interest for your membership site is to create teaser content and distribute it using different online channels such as:

- Blogs: Blog posts tend to attract an audience of people eager to learn more about a topic. Therefore, create a series of blog posts that include calls to action. Pointing your blog post to your webinar promoting your membership site will drive considerable amounts of free traffic.

- Webinars: A webinar is a great opportunity to showcase your membership site. You offer one hour of incredibly valuable information. Then you offer the option for people to further their education by joining your subscription-based content. It's an easy way to turn webinar attendees into subscription-based customers.

- YouTube videos: Youtube.com has become the second most-visited website on the web. Create a YouTube channel to host teaser videos that also point to the sales video of your membership site. This could generate a significant amount of traffic.

- Social media: Two billion people are currently using one or more social platforms to connect and exchange information. Therefore, if you tap into this traffic source, chances are you'll be able to reach potential customers.

The traditional way of using social media as a marketer, is to publish a post with a link to your sales material. An even more effective way is to allow other people to do it for you. Since marketing on social media requires you to have an existing audience—which you may or may not have—allowing social sharing on your blog and email enables you to turn your existing traffic into word-of-mouth traffic. Each social media user has, on average, 140 contacts in their network. If you add social sharing tabs below your blog posts, or remind webinar attendees and video viewers to share your content, this can increase your traffic—and therefore your sales—exponentially.

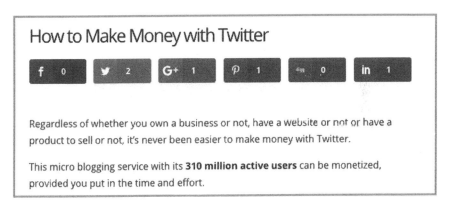

How to Make Money with Twitter

Regardless of whether you own a business or not, have a website or not or have a product to sell or not, it's never been easier to make money with Twitter.

This micro blogging service with its **310 million active users** can be monetized, provided you put in the time and effort.

4. Set up a sales-processing facility.
   To process sales for subscription-based products, merchant facilities such as paypal.com allow you to create recurring payment links.

- <u>Create a Subscription button</u> ⬅
- <u>Create an Add to Cart button</u>
- <u>Create a Buy Now button</u>
- <u>Create a Donate button</u>
- <u>Create a Buy Gift Voucher button</u>
- <u>Sign up for Enhanced Recurring Payments</u>
- <u>Go to My saved buttons</u>

PayPal also enables you to automate a big section of customer service. It allows you to send an email confirmation automatically. This would send your customers their membership access details upon completing their payment.

If you already have an online merchant facility, other services such as 1shoppingcart.com and infusionsoft.com also allow you to create recurring payment links and set up automated email confirmations.

Email confirmations should include the following:

- Confirmation of their subscription level
- Details on how to access their membership
- Customer support contact details

Here's an example of an email confirmation for membership-site customers:

Dear name,

Congratulations for becoming a valued member of NAME OF PRODUCT

During our time together we'll work very closely with you so you can master the skill of XYZ.

To give you all the support you need, we're giving you complete access to our private membership website exclusive to students and current members paying $97 per month.

In order to access your members' area, register your account and select a password here:
http://internetcoachingschool.com/?/register/XYZ

This website features all the training material you need on XYZ

Should you require further support, please don't hesitate to email us at support@yourwebsite.com

To your success,

Your name

---

5. Price your membership.
   For most membership sites, prices tend to remain below $100 a month. Although there is no specific rule when it comes to pricing, as it can fluctuate significantly according to the topic, the industry, the competition and the target audience, testing different prices is the best way to proceed.

At first, put your monthly fee at any price below $100, and as people start buying, closely monitor your conversion rate. If your conversion rate is below ten per cent, start putting the price down or add more value to make your offer even more irresistible. If your conversion rate is above ten per cent, increase the price until you hit a ten per cent conversion rate.

Once you've secured a few monthly paying subscribers, the key to your financial success will be to keep them subscribed for as long as possible. A lot of membership site owners will tell you that the average 'stick rate' is three months, which means that you'll have to keep putting effort into acquiring customers.

However there are a few ways you can limit member cancelations. These include:

- Putting an end date on the membership. If the expiry date of the subscription is stated clearly during the sales process, members tend to wait for the subscription to expire instead of canceling it.

- Over-deliver on your promises. Always adding fresh, new content that members are unlikely to find anywhere else, will enable customers to justify to themselves that their money is well spent. The key when sharing content is to include pieces of information that trigger 'aha' moments. People love discovering new things and especially enjoy knowing things most people don't know. When you become that source of information, customer retention gets much easier.

- Whet your members' appetite with what is coming up next. Email your members a few days before they get billed for next month's access and include a reminder of what is ahead. This will almost certainly guarantee to hook your members in.

- Constantly engage with your members. To increase engagement with your subscribers, simply add and monitor a forum that is exclusive to them. You can also include a question submission form within the members' area and ensure any questions are answered within 24 hours. Fast and helpful customer support goes a long way when it comes to membership retention. In addition, hold live monthly calls with further teaching. Including a Q and A session will also ensure that subscribers remain engaged, and therefore loyal.

- If a cancelation looks inevitable, think of including a downsell option. Members paying $97 for information and wishing to cancel are easier to convert into $27 customers than acquiring a new prospect. An automated email saying, "We're sorry to see you go, and would like to offer you the opportunity to remain a member for only $27 (without access to customer support) as a thank you for your continued support," can turn cancellations into more recurring income streams.

It is always easier and cheaper to generate sales from an existing customer than to acquire a new one. Increasing your stick rate should be your number one priority.

CASE STUDY: MARK ANASTASI

Mark Anastasi (online entrepreneur, New York Times bestselling author and my brother-in-law!) started his journey online by selling eBooks. After he discovered the power of webinars, he implemented the Loop strategy to monetize them further. Mark simply integrated "Amember" (membership management software which allows users to accept subscription payments, manage member profiles and share content) and 2checkout (an online payment processing service) with his website.

The approach Mark followed to attract members was simple. He offered a $5 trial membership for 30 days and then charged $97 a month. Members received recordings of his seminars—Mark runs some of the biggest web business education seminars in Europe—bonus courses, and one live group-coaching webinar a month. In the webinar, which he'd teach exclusively to members, he'd cover one new marketing, traffic-generation or income-generation strategy.

To launch his membership service, Mark ran two free, live webinars where he taught web business strategies. Then he offered his $5, 30-day trial. His two free webinars secured him 220 trial members and over the course of 12 months, the membership dwindled to 80 core members, which brought in over $100,000 in revenue (95 per cent of which was pure profit).

Mark recommends implementing the Loop strategy in three stages.
- Stage one. Focus on building your mailing list and establishing rapport with email subscribers. Do this by sending regular, useful newsletters.

- Stage two. Create multiple $97 information products and store them in your membership site.
- Stage three. To attract more members, run free webinars to your list offering one of your $97 products or a $5, 30-day trial to access everything.

MONEY ON DEMAND

CHAPTER 9

JV BROKER

A few years into using webinars as the main sales vehicle for my Internet business—and teaching others to do the same—it surprised me that more people were not using the technology to sell more products.

I realized that the main reason people weren't using webinars as a sales vehicle, was their lack of confidence to present. The assumption that 'you have to have the gift of the gab to be able to talk for an hour' was stopping people from leveraging the power of webinars.

Another reason people don't use webinars is the thought of having to sell. Selling is a daunting task, and most people prefer not to do it.

Do you hate selling too?

If so, the JV broker strategy is a very exciting business model for you. You don't have to present a webinar, sell a webinar or even market a webinar, and you can still profit by becoming a webinar JV broker.

All that a JV broker needs to do is to link list owners with webinar owners and negotiate a deal where each person involved gets a cut.

In other words, with the JV Broker strategy, you bring a webinar owner and a list owner together and get a cut.

What makes this such a powerful strategy, is that you don't have to build a mailing list or put together a webinar. A webinar JV broker can literally start generating cash flow within days.

The main skills required to be a sought-after JV broker are networking, negotiating, and the ability to build relationships with key people.

JV broker — Becoming the invisible hand

1. Locate a webinar owner.
   Businesses who use webinars as a sales vehicle are always looking for more traffic and more exposure to their webinars.
   Social media is most probably the fastest way to locate webinar owners, as they often promote their webinars on social media.
   Use the built-in search engines that exist on social media. If you type 'webinar' into the search box, it will instantly list all the posts that contain the keyword 'webinar'.

2. Contact the business owner

You can contact them directly on social media.
Facebook, for example, allows you to message people
whether or not you're connected to them.
Alternatively, you can contact them through their
website.

If the webinar owner has secretaries or assistants, it
might require a few more attempts until you can
secure a meeting with the decision maker.

A typical message can look like this:

Hello [Firstname],

I hope you're well. I'm a big fan of your work!

My name is [Your Name] and I'd like to discuss the opportunity of sharing your webinars with hundreds—if not thousands—more people.

I've helped several business owners, in similar industries to yours, tap into larger audiences, and increase their sales dramatically, by putting them in touch with list owners. I'm confident I can help you achieve the same with your webinars.

Would you be interested in scheduling a call to discuss this further?

I look forward to hearing from you.

Kind regards,
[Your Name]

The first message should be short, and should emphasize how you can help them generate more sales. No business owner would decline an opportunity to talk further about how they can increase their sales, so get ready to schedule lots of calls.

3. Phone the business owner
    If emails and messages don't lead to any response, pick up the phone. In the first phone call, your aim is to schedule a ten-minute conversation, either in person or over the phone. Don't try to pitch your business proposal during an unsolicited call. It leaves a bad impression.

    Instead open the conversation by saying:

"Hi firstname,

My name's John, and I've been watching your webinars. I'd like to discuss the opportunity of dramatically increasing your sales. I know I'm interrupting your day right now, so would you like to schedule some time for a meeting or a call? It's going to take just ten minutes, and I can show you how all this can work, without you putting any time or effort into it."

The above is a much more effective option.

One mistake people make when pitching a business opportunity is to make the conversation about their offer, instead of about how the business owner can generate more sales.
Another error is to discuss how money will be split before getting a firm indication that the business owner is even interested.

4. Send a proposal
   When there's a firm indication from a business owner that they're willing to give up a percentage of the sales generated in exchange for more exposure, the next step is to send a written proposal. In that, you stress that the terms of the proposal can be negotiated. By putting together a written proposal it not only shows you're serious but it will also differentiate you from others.

Most people never put together written proposals and since most people in business get flooded with opportunities. The ones that usually stand out and get considered are the ones from people who take the time to put their idea in writing.

In the first draft of the proposal, you educate the business owner about your responsibilities as the JV broker, and their responsibility as the webinar owner. This starts the JV process and avoids costly misunderstandings.

A JV broker proposal can look like this:

AGREEMENT BETWEEN .... AND ....

The Promotion:

Country:

Duration: Ongoing contract

JV Broker:

Email Address:

Webinar JV partner:

In signing this agreement, the JV broker and webinar JV partner agree to the following:

AGREEMENT: This agreement provides the JV broker with the right to broker JV promotional deals on behalf of, and only with pre-approval of each deal, the webinar JV partner for the promotion of webinars in COUNTRY, for the duration of the agreement. The JV broker is effectively a contractor to the webinar JV partner.

COLLATERAL: The JV broker will be provided with marketing material by the webinar JV partner in written, video and image format relating to The Promotion, to forward onto approved list owners.

PARTNERSHIP: It is agreed that JV broker and webinar JV partner will work closely together in order to create the best results possible on each promotion and feedback on results is welcome from each party. All will be carried out in consultation with and approval from the JV partner.

APPEARANCE: The agreement represents webinar appearance of NAME OF BUSINESS OR NAME OF BUSINESS OWNER.

BRANDING: The JV broker will comply with branding guidelines in promotional and marketing material, and ensure that if changed, material for marketing campaigns is submitted and approved prior to execution where possible (keeping in mind list owners may change copy themselves without notifying JV broker).

EXPENSES: All expenses relating to the pre-promotion preparation, delivery of the promotion and post delivery of services, follow up of sales and payments including all expenses related to promotion are all the responsibility of the webinar JV partner.

INCOME and EARNINGS: The JV broker will receive ten per cent of the sales generated from the webinar with the list owner provided. No additional payments relating to holiday or sick leave, etc. are payable to the JV broker.

These commissions will be paid to the JV broker within six weeks of any promotion they apply to, to the account listed on the invoice.

JV Broker OBLIGATIONS

The JV Manager agrees to:
a. Identify potential list owners with right target market and make them known to webinar JV partner to choose from.

b. Organize approved (by JV partner) Promotion, delivering a minimum of one JV per month.

c. Manage all payments to list owners.

d. Manage the effective communications to all applicable approved JV partners ensuring timely mail-outs.

e. Ensure promotional content is provided to the list owner on the dates agreed by both parties.

f. Approach new potential list owners that the webinar JV partner wishes to work with. These are to be made known to the JV broker each month.

g. Request that the database of approved list owners comprises quality leads i.e. qualified, up to date, working email addresses.

Webinar JV Partner OBLIGATIONS AND RESPONSIBILITIES:

a. Agree to send promotional material for any approved and applicable promotions for list owners engaged by JV broker on dates negotiated and agreed upon in writing.

The creation of marketing materials and campaigns to effectively capture and enroll potential leads and to be provided to JV broker in a timely manner.

b. Full responsibility for all sales and future delivery of the programs and products sold at The Promotion.

c. Provide JV broker with an affiliate link for each promotion.

d. Management, reporting and tracking of JV broker's affiliate link made from The Promotional deals brokered by JV broker and all applicable resulting payments to the JV broker and list owner.

e. This agreement will remain confidential, to be discussed only by JV broker and webinar JV partner.

f. The list owners introduced by the JV broker will remain clients of the JV broker to be engaged by JV broker for any future promotions on behalf of webinar JV partner.

A report from list owners' sales will be provided to JV broker to show resulting sales from each JV promotional deal brokered.

Signed: _____

Name: Date:

Signed: _____

Name: Date:

5. Contact a list owner

   Use a similar process to secure a deal with a list owner. The only difference is, you'll need to sell the idea of them generating more revenue from their existing audience while not having to deliver additional products or provide further customer support.

CASE STUDY: COLLEEN WOODSTOCK

Colleen Woodstock has been implementing The JV Broker strategy very successfully for the past few years.

She started her career as a corporate sales executive, where she mastered negotiation and sales skills. After working for a few years in the corporate world, she realized she had the skills to start a consulting business.

Her first consulting client was an international speaker and event promoter for whom she helped to fill events thanks to joint ventures. Her client base of event promoters and speakers grew steadily, and she was soon helping a large network of businesses to fill their events and increase their webinar attendance rates for a percentage of the sales generated.

Colleen now makes a full-time living working from home as a JV broker. She works just two days a week and dedicates the rest of her time to her family.

To find list owners and product owners, she first looks for people who inspire her, and whose work she admires. She attends events and subscribes to various newsletters. She finds that working with people who inspire her is highly motivating, so this has been her main selection criterion throughout the years. She also keeps an eye out in her email inbox to discover 'who is doing what'. This is another good source of potential partners. When she identifies potential partners, she researches them online and subscribes to their newsletter. She uses LinkedIn to get in touch with them.

Her secret weapon in the JV Broker strategy, is to build relationships before proposing anything. Never go in cold. She shapes her proposals based on whatever solution each partner wants.

According to Colleen, you should spend time building relationships (which can include buying the potential partner's products and engaging with them as a customer). You then find out what solutions they want (by asking the right questions). Then, as you're offering a solution to their problems, it's hard for anyone to turn you down.

CHAPTER 10

PRODUCTIZATION

One of the biggest hurdles people feel they need to overcome, before putting together a webinar, is having a product to sell. If you don't have a product to sell, how can you sell it on a webinar?

So they turn to affiliate marketing (marketing other people's products for a commission) or multi-level. People think, "If I have a product, I can sell it and make money".
However, the reality is, having a product to sell does not guarantee any sales. It's the process you take people through in order to close the sale that makes or breaks a business. This is why people can sell below-average products and still create income. By the same token, people who own products that could completely transform people's lives for the better, might never manage to close a single sale.

It's the process you take people through that will make or break your ability to generate profits, and not the product itself.

You don't need to have a product prior to putting together a webinar. In fact, selling on a webinar a product that does not yet exist is one of the best practices. Your customers may actually prefer it that way.

It's no surprise that when looking at Robert Kiyosaki's B-I triangle—his model for building the most successful businesses—products are placed in the smallest portion of the B-I triangle.

The world is full of high quality products, but proven processes to sell them are rare.

The winning formula for sales is a perfectly crafted sales process and a quality product that solves a problem.

So how do webinars fit into this equation?

When you sell a product that hasn't been created on a webinar, we call it the Money-On-Demand Productization. In other words, you're selling more webinars at the end of a webinar. You don't have to spend time creating a product, or spend money buying stock unless it sells.

If you don't have a product, you can simply sell more webinars!

You package webinar information into webinar series of four, eight, ten or twelve webinars, and this creates the perfect product. (N.B. More than twelve webinars could be packaged into advanced series.)

People attend a 60-minute or 90-minute webinar because they have a hunger to learn about the topic covered. A percentage of those people (usually ten per cent) want to go further, faster by learning more. What better way to teach them more than by delivering further webinars?

The beauty of this method is threefold.
First, you don't have to create anything or fork out large sums of money to acquire products before they actually sell—and if you don't sell anything you don't have to do anything.
Secondly, it's a great market research tool, allowing you to gather critical data from a small number of people that can be used to shape the rest of your business.
Thirdly, the webinar series doesn't have to be produced and delivered upfront.

We usually recommend that people who opt for this strategy deliver each subsequent webinar on a weekly basis, using a live and interactive broadcast platform such as gotowebinar.com.

From our experience, most customers prefer this delivery method, as they can engage and interact with the expert directly, and ask questions while they're being taught.

These live webinars can, of course, be recorded for future customers, allowing the product owner to leverage their time.

Productization — Creating products only after you've sold them

1. Give a name to your product.
   For example, if your initial webinar was about *How to lose five pounds a month*, you could name your product, *the weight loss acceleration eight-week program*.

2. List the webinars (also known as "modules") included in the program.
   For example, *the weight loss acceleration eight-week program* could include the following webinars:

   • Webinar 1: How to calculate your ideal weight
   • Webinar 2: How to read food labels
   • Webinar 3: How to clean your fridge and pantry
   • Webinar 4: How to create meal plans
   • Webinar 5: How to speed up your metabolism
   • Webinar 6: The foods that make you feel full for longer
   • Webinar 7: The food combination method for weight loss
   • Webinar 8: How to maintain your ideal weight

3. State the total value of the webinar series package.
   This could range from a few hundred dollars to a few thousand dollars. Price your product below its total value. For example, should the total value be $500, you could sell your yet-to-be-created product series

at $297, making it a no-brainer decision for potential customers.

How do you work out the value of something that isn't created yet? There are a number of ways to do this. The most common way is to look at what other people in your industry are charging. By including the value of every element included in your product, you're raising the perceived value of your overall product to your prospects. If you don't add a value as you itemize your offer, the prospect will think it's not worth anything at all.

To increase the value of the package, and therefore increase the price of the product, it's advisable to either add more webinars or offer additional items such as one-on-one coaching, consulting, templates, check lists, etc. For example,

The Weight Loss Acceleration Eight-Week Program could also include:

- Six 30-minute telephone consultations – value $297
- A calorie counter log – value $97
- A diet health checklist – value $47
- Access to a private Facebook support group – valued $97
- A portion size guide – value $47
- An interview with a weight-loss expert – value $297
- Case studies of successful people – value $97
- Etc. ...

The list could go on and on. The key is to include items that are either quick to put together or already available, and that complement the core package—the webinar series. It's poor business practice to add irrelevant items as bonuses to justify the price.

4. Use the Money-On-Demand Productization strategy as a market research tool.
   You can test how warm a market is to your idea and also find the right price structure.

Too many people fall into the trap of surveying friends or family, which are, on most occasions, not the target audience. The feedback you receive from acquaintances is not as valuable as feedback from someone who has parted with their money for your offer.

When people implement the Money-On-Demand Productization strategy for the first time, we strongly recommend that they add one-on-one consulting into their package. Although, at first, it might appear hard to sustain if faced with many buyers, our experience shows that most customers never request the calls. It's sad that we live in such a wasteful society. People buy books they never read, clothes they never wear, food they throw away and do university and college courses they never get a career in. They buy gym memberships they never use, courses they don't follow through, and coaching programs they never complete.

Some customers request just one call. That initial call has proven critical in the success of a business, as it is an opportunity for the product owner to survey customers, and ask the key question:
"What made you buy the product?"

The answers that customers provide will enable you to understand the main pain point of your audience (what is the main problem they're trying to solve). You can also discover what it was in your package that was their tipping point for making the buying decision.

Further information such as your customer avatar can also be gathered within that first call. This will become invaluable when fine-tuning your marketing message and targeting your customers.

You can also survey customers about the price of your product.

CASE STUDY: SEAN ALLISON

Sean Allison (ex-government employee from Perth) had considerable experience with options trading and had made a fair bit of money from trading options in his spare time. When he decided to sell an options trading course on his first webinar, he priced it at $997 for a series of eight webinars and some one-on-one calls. Remember, the series hadn't been created yet. He was listing what he would deliver for $997 in the future.

He used it very effectively as a market research tool. To his surprise, the main response he received to the question, "What made you buy the product?" was, "We bought it because your strategy didn't require us to sell anything to anyone in order to produce income." This helped him to improve his lead-generation method. He included the headline, 'The little-known strategy for producing income that doesn't require you to sell anything to anyone' in his marketing material.

An additional gem of information concerned the price of his product. When he asked how his customers felt about his $997 price for packaged webinars and six one-one-calls, the answer was, from almost every customer, "It's way below the price of other options-trading courses, and they don't offer as much as you."

Since most of his competitors were pricing their courses around $7,000 and more, Sean put the price up to $4,997 and to this day it remains the most competitive price.

Sean's business, which started with the Money-On-Demand Productization strategy is now, four years later, a multi-million-dollar enterprise.

As I said earlier, it's unfortunate that people buy things they never use, so don't take it personally when people pay you lots of money and then never call or study your programs or use your products or service at all.

I have a different perspective. This first occurred to me when I was working with a student and business partner who was selling a property-investing training program. He'd sold his program to eight customers at $997 on his first webinar. Then he delivered eight weekly webinars, six one-on-one coaching calls delivered via Skype, unlimited customer support by email and some extra bonuses as well.

He delivered one webinar per week as he'd promised and completed the eight weeks. Then he phoned me saying, "Steven, there's something wrong. Only one of my customers has succeeded." The customer had purchased 22 properties as a result of implementing his course in a very short amount of time. (These were cheap blocks of land and houses in the US ranging from $2000 to $20,000.)

I said, "That's great! You got one testimonial from your first course!" I saw it as a great success. He was surprised that nobody used the six Skype coaching calls—I think he said a few had one or two calls with him. I assured him that it's normal that people buy things they don't use right now, but he was still uneasy and I could sense he really cared. This is an important trait that I consider a necessity if I'm to partner with someone. So I suggested that he call them and say, "Hey, I'm just calling to see how you're going with the program and ask if you'd like to book a Skype call because you're entitled to six."

Everyone who answered from the seven people thanked him for calling, said how much they loved the program, but explained that they'd been busy or had some other excuse as to why they hadn't bought a property or used the coaching calls with him.

He called me back and said, "Steven, you were right. They're just busy."

Another month passed and he called me again. He said they still hadn't called. I assured him that THERE WAS NOTHING WRONG WITH HIS PROGRAM.

"Do you think that when they signed up for your course at $997 they wanted to buy a property?" I asked him.

He thought they did, and life just got in the way for them. I asked him if there was another way he could help them reach their desire to get a property? I suggested maybe he could find, secure and purchase the property for them.

He agreed that he could do that, and walked me through the process and told me how long it would take. I asked him how much he'd charge for all of that. He wasn't sure. I asked if he'd do it for $10,000 and he said he would.

I told him to phone the seven customers who hadn't used his program and hadn't made any progress yet to ask them what was holding them up. I also told Sean to ask them in particular if they need any help and to justify the call by adding, "because so many people want to buy a property using my methods but life has gotten in the way, I've created a complete done-for-you package where I search, find, put in an offer and purchase the property for you, (plus some extras)—and I charge $10,000 to do it all."

One of the seven customers he spoke to that day negotiated a slight discount and (from memory) deposited $8000 or

$9000 into his bank account. It took him a day to do the work and his "profit-maker" high end product was born.

He had just made more money from one customer than he had made from the other seven. That business model alone is a million-dollar business.

I always recommend that people include at least six one-on-one consulting calls on the first ever webinar, when the product hasn't been created yet, for three reasons:

1. To ensure that customers become successful
2. To collect testimonials for future webinars
3. To work out what additional products or services these customers will want

I call this process: "getting paid for market research".

Most people I share this strategy with are reluctant at first to implement it, and often say to me, "Steven, adding one-on-one consulting calls is so time consuming, are you crazy? For only $297? I earn that (or more) in an hour!"

But if you think about it, the first time you're creating a program or product or course—to have people on the phone with you, helping them, getting their feedback live as you're creating it, is the number one most valuable market research ever. And you're getting paid to do it.

I always obtain my most useful feedback from people who've invested in a program or product of mine. I only listen to buyers—not 'spectating prospects' or 'spec-pects' as I call them!

MONEY ON DEMAND

CHAPTER 11

B2B

With the continuing growth in popularity for webinars, more and more businesses are looking to add webinars to their marketing channel or as part of their sales funnel. Since webinars cost next-to-nothing to produce, the return on investment can be almost immediate. This also means that there is a growing demand from businesses for services that can facilitate the process of producing, promoting, and even managing ongoing webinars.

There are two types of businesses that would benefit greatly from using webinars:

1. A business looking either to generate more leads in a more cost effective way, or looking to sell one-to-many instead of one-to-one.

   For example, a business consultant who has been selling his services by cold-calling and one-on-one appointments could leverage his time by delivering a webinar to hundreds (if not thousands) of people simultaneously and selling his services at the end of it.
   Or a website development company could leverage webinars by putting together a free webinar titled *How to create websites that convert into sales* to attract leads interested in website design

information, then offer their website development services.

2. The other type of business that would benefit greatly from adding webinars in their business model, is a business with remote teams who need to be managed and trained, which can represent a significant ongoing cost. Making sure that these teams remain motivated and productive is also a challenge. Most remote teams fail to produce consistent results, because their members don't have sufficient opportunity to communicate and collaborate with each other. The lack of connection between team members and the absence of team culture can make remote projects fall apart. Although the productivity of remote teams can be restored through proper on-site management, it's not as cost effective as using webinars for management.

By using webinars to manage remote teams, virtual meetings can be scheduled at no extra cost. In addition, team members can talk to each other, see each other, share their screens, and deliver presentations from their work location all while under the supervision of management.
Webinars not only increase the productivity and motivation of remote teams, they can also help to hold them accountable and create opportunities to feel connected as a team.
Webinars can also be used in such companies as a hiring and training tool. For example, many people we hired in our businesses to work remotely, were interviewed via webinar and later trained via webinar.

So webinars can be used not only as a cost effective leads-and sales-generator but also as a cost effective management tool.

Since many businesses need to improve either their sales or their management processes, the Money-On-Demand B2B strategy can be a highly lucrative business model.

The Money-On-Demand B2B business strategy is either:

- The process of getting paid upfront for every webinar you produce for a business.
  or
- Getting paid on an ongoing basis for ongoing webinars you set up on business' behalf.

B2B — Playing with the big boys

1. Find customers.
   There are three ways to do this:

Online

Create a sophisticated sales funnel with:
  I. A lead capture page: a web page asking for people to submit their contact details in exchange for a free offer.

LEAD GENERATION 2.0

The Best "Newly Discovered" Lead And Sales Generation Tactic On Twitter

Inside you'll learn:

1. How to syphon unlimited targeted leads in any niche thanks to Twitter.

2. The secret code no one wants you to know to identify targeted leads already asking to buy your products.

3. Exactly what to do on Twitter so your leads turn into raving fans and customer.

4. The little-known 3-step system to generate leads and sales without spending a cent on advertising.

Click Here - It's FREE

Get My FREE eBook Now

II. A 'mouse trap' page: a page where prospects would land after submitting their contact details, where you'd offer a small upsell (five to ten dollars) to weed out the buyers from the freebie-seekers.

STEVEN AND CORINNA ESSA

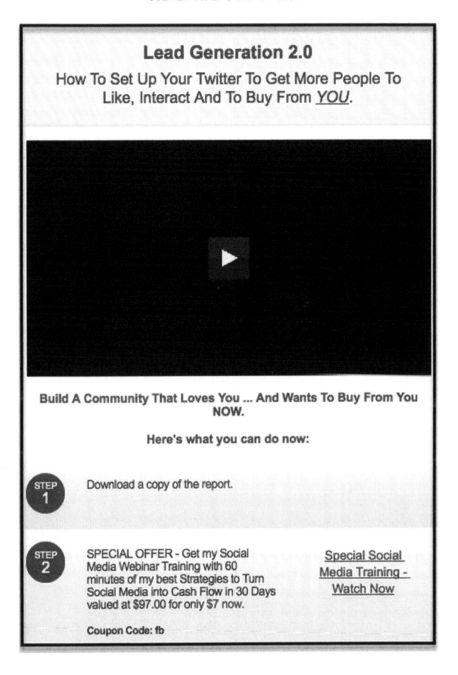

III. A 'main offer' page: a page where you'd introduce and offer your done-for-you services.

Using the online method requires skills in traffic generation and copywriting, and the patience to split test, track and optimize. If done correctly, however, it can be an extremely efficient and cost effective way to get customers fast.

Offline

- Tap into your existing network (if you have one) and ask for referrals.
- Ask highly qualified face-to-face sales people to do some cold calling.

The key when following the offline method is to hire a sales manager who would be responsible for hiring the sales people and keeping them motivated and incentivized enough to reach their targets.

Attraction

The preferred method is to have customers knock on your door without you having to perform any sophisticated sales or marketing techniques.

The easiest way to do this is to choose an industry where webinars would represent considerable leverage, and position yourself as a webinar expert by conducting your own webinars for that industry.

2. Setting up the webinars.

Single Webinar Set Up

To set up a single webinar for a business, follow the step-by-step process below:

1. Put together the slides for the business' webinar using the template: introduction – content – close
2. Write the pitch if they want to use the webinar to generate sales
3. Customize the slides if they wish to add branding to their content
4. Schedule the webinar
5. Add-on services could include:
   a. Promoting the webinar (putting together marketing material such as email broadcasts, press releases and social media ads)
   b. Recording the webinar
   c. Editing the webinar recording

d. Creating the webinar replay
e. Co-hosting the webinar
f. Attending the live webinar to trouble-shoot any technical glitches
g. Presenting the webinar

Multiple webinar set up

When creating multiple webinars on behalf of businesses, follow the step-by-step process below. Remember, charging a business for multiple webinars at once will cost the business less than buying webinars individually. This option can also serve as an easy upsell for businesses willing to pay you upfront to test multiple webinars.

1. Put together the slides for the business' webinar using the template: introduction – content - close
2. Write the pitch if they want to use the webinar to generate sales
3. Customize the slides if they wish to add branding to their content
4. Schedule the webinar
5. Add-on services could include:
   a. Promoting the webinar (putting together marketing material such as email broadcasts, press releases and social media ads)
   b. Recording the webinar
   c. Editing the webinar recording
   d. Creating the webinar replay
   e. Co-hosting the webinar
   f. Attending the live webinar to trouble-shoot any technical glitches
   g. Presenting the webinar

Recurring webinar set up

This level of service is perfect for businesses looking to run a minimum of one webinar a month, or for businesses wanting to use webinars for staff management.

1. Put the slides together
2. Schedule the webinar
3. Send email invitations to team members to attend the webinar
4. Send email reminders
5. Record the webinar
6. Edit the webinar recording
7. Send out or store the replay

If you display the three levels of done-for-you services, this shows all the options available and makes the upsell and downsell process much easier and natural. It creates the opportunity to design customized quotes for businesses wanting a combination of all three levels of service.

When you display the three levels of done-for-you services, make one stand out (usually the mid-range level of service) as the "most popular" service. Too much choice can confuse people—and 'a confused mind almost never buys'— so when one of the services stands out, it can speed up the decision   process.

CASE STUDY: KAREN BONNANO

Karen Bonnano, one of my students, started an education consultancy business in the 90s, specializing in providing classroom teachers with professional learning, to update what they were taught at university. This involved considerable time travelling and staying in motels.

When Karen discovered webinars, she put together her modules as a webinar presentation and promoted them using social media, her existing contacts and discussion lists of teachers.

Karen was in the Australian education industry, where it is compulsory for teachers to have a number of professional learning hours annually in order to retain their teaching registration. Nobody likes to travel unnecessarily, so this made webinars and Karen's services in demand.

Webinar technology allowed Karen to deliver multiple trainings in a single day without leaving her house:

"I remember once, on a Saturday morning, I was delivering training to a group of educators in the USA and at 2pm, I was teaching a group of educators in Tasmania— without leaving my house. I got my life back," she recalls.

Her first paid webinar was launched in May 2011 and generated $700 in sales.

Webinar technology has also allowed Karen to multiply her income by five while working less.

Soon after she established herself as the go-to person for professional learning, people in her industry started knocking at her door requesting her help with putting together webinars.

The first call she received was from the marketing manager for *Google Education* who offered to pay Karen $1,700 to set up a webinar for their company.

One of Karen's main sources of income is the Money-On-Demand B2B strategy, where she now has five-figure clients knocking at her door for her services. When asked how customers feel about her upfront fees, she answered, "Paying a few thousand dollars to have a webinar put together for them is a drop in the ocean considering how many leads it will generate—compared to the cost of generating leads through advertising."

MONEY ON DEMAND

CHAPTER 12

INTERVIEW

Although selling on a webinar can give anyone leverage (webinars convert at ten per cent if not more), people are still reluctant to sell after delivering a 45-minute presentation. For many, the idea of 'pitching' conjures up visions of ruthless, greedy and manipulative sales people. They'd rather be hit by a bus than be associated with people like that! So no matter how much value the presentation delivered, no matter how much the product or service can help people's lives for the better, and no matter how good the value of the product or service—when it comes to delivering the close, presenters lose their enthusiasm. Their tone of voice becomes unassertive and their whole demeanor during the sales process becomes apprehensive.

It's important to note that if you deliver great information on a webinar and then don't sell something or offer something, the ten per cent who would usually buy will now be ready to run with your information and be looking elsewhere to buy something from someone else. I always say, I trust my products more than I trust my competition, and I'd rather you bought my program than someone else's.

I believe that to deliver great value for free before you sell is a great win/win situation. Remember—you aren't holding someone at gunpoint to stay on your webinar, they can leave anytime at the end when you're offering your product. Never apologize for selling something, especially when you've delivered great value first for the majority of the webinar. Don't use tricks, though. Many people try to employ Neuro-Linguistic Programming (NLP) and other forms of manipulation. I don't. I say, keep it simple, be yourself, deliver great content and the rest will look after itself.

Not maintaining the same tone of voice during the close, or the same level of enthusiasm and passion, will jeopardize— if not kill—any chance of making sales. Closing sales is the process of transferring one person's enthusiasm to another person, so doing this poorly is a surefire way to stop sales from coming through.

However, anyone whose stomach turns at the idea of selling anything to anyone will love the Money-On-Demand Interview strategy. This method of generating money (and a lot of it) involves interviewing experts on a webinar about their products and services.

Although it doesn't fit the standard formula of: information + pitch = sales, it has turned experts into millionaires. Robert Kiyosaki, for example, was interviewed by Oprah Winfrey to discuss his book *Rich Dad, Poor Dad*. He sold millions of copies as a direct result of the interview. In fact, not only does an expert benefit from being interviewed, so does the interviewer! Some of the richest people on the planet such as Oprah Winfrey and Michael Parkinson are interviewers.

Although interviews are the equivalent of long sales presentations, they don't appear that way, and this makes the selling process effective and effortless. It puts any expert wanting to generate revenue from their knowledge at ease.

There is not much difference between a standard webinar and an interview. The main difference is that the webinar is punctuated by someone asking questions, rather than a presenter going through the presentation alone.

Interviews — The Oprah Winfrey formula

1. Find an expert
   There are many experts in the world, eager for more exposure, and it's never been easier to get in touch with them.

   - Websites such as expertclick.com can put you in touch with a range of different experts
   - Companies such as interviewconnections.com can put you in contact with experts of your choice in exchange for a fee
   - Amazon.com lists all the authors in a given industry

   Getting in touch with them is as easy as connecting with them on social media or sending them an email through their website.

   An expert will easily agree to be interviewed if you offer a network of people they can tap into. If you have thousands of social media followers, or a large mailing list, or thousands of YouTube subscribers, this can easily entice experts to agree to an interview. In addition, if all you ask is for a percentage of the sales generated as a result of the interview, and no upfront costs, it means that there is no cost and no risks involved for them.

2. Structure the interview

The structure of the interview is the same as the structure of a webinar:

- The introduction. The presenter or expert has the opportunity to position themselves as an authority figure.
- The content. The presenter or expert delivers information while illustrating the points with examples, case studies, and stories.
- The close. The presenter or expert offers an opportunity to the attendees to learn more, reach their goals faster or eliminate their problems by using the product or service, while also answering common sales objections.

An interview also follows this pattern.

The first two or three questions should invite the expert to introduce themselves and position themselves as experts. This part is no longer than ten or fifteen minutes. It doesn't try to sell anything because you don't want attendees to have their guards up. You want to build trust and rapport.

1. How did you become such an expert in xyz?
2. How has your information/expertise/experience helped people?
3. Do you have specific examples of people whose life has changed thanks to your knowledge?

The next part of the interview should invite the interviewee to share some knowledge and expertise. It should last about 30 minutes, and give listeners clear instructions and guidelines on what to do to achieve the result promised by the expert. The interviewer's responsibility is to make sure that the expert doesn't use any jargon that is likely to confuse listeners, and to ensure that the information shared is enough for people to implement, whether or not they buy the product. Lastly, if the information shared is complex, the interviewer's job is either to re-iterate what has been said, or ask the expert to illustrate it with clear examples.

The following questions will help extract that information:

1. So, what steps should someone follow to achieve xyz?
2. What are the common challenges people are likely to face when following these steps?
3. What are the best practices in order to ensure success in xyz?
4. How long would it take someone to achieve xyz?
5. What is likely to stop people from achieving xyz?
6. What are the common mistakes people make when trying to achieve xyz?

The last part of the interview is where the interviewee has an opportunity to talk about their product or service. The following questions will give the listeners enough information about the features and benefits and also offer an opportunity for a strong call to action.

Question 10 should act as a transition between parts two and three of the webinar, the same way a webinar presentation would have a slide to transition between the content and the close. Question 10 should also be an opportunity to discuss the features of the product or service, such as the name of the product and its format (a book, an online course, etc....)

1. You've created (name of the product or service); can you tell us more about it?
2. How can (name of the product or service) help people in achieving XYZ (benefit of the product or service)?
   This question provides the opportunity to mention the benefits of the product or service. It shouldn't be rushed. Mentioning the benefits is the most important part of the close.
3. How fast can people achieve XYZ (benefit of the product or service) as a result of getting hold of (name of the product or service)?
   This question is not applicable in all circumstances, but if the product or service can lead to specific results faster, it is important to mention this.
4. What was your customer's experience after they purchased (name of product or service)?
   This question is the equivalent of the testimonials in a normal webinar. It allows the interviewee to share endorsements that have been received.
5. For the people listening to this webinar, do you have a special offer for them?
   This adds an element of urgency, which is critical in any selling environment. Always give a special bonus such as a discount or a free gift to push listeners to buy now rather than later. To create even greater urgency, the expert could say that the bonus is only available for the first ten people, for example.
6. Where can people purchase (name of product or service)?

This is the call to action. It explains clearly where people can complete their purchase.

If the interviewer is familiar with the expert's product and has had a positive experience as a result of using it, this is the part of the interview where you can say this. For example, for a weight loss program, the interviewer could say,

"I've personally struggled with my weight for a long time, I've tried lots and lots of diets, and your program has made a huge difference as I've lost 12 pounds in a month and I've managed to keep the weight off. I couldn't recommend you higher."

If the interviewer has built a rapport with the listeners, endorsing the product personally can make a tremendous amount of difference in terms of conversions.

3. Rehearse the interview first and transcribe it. This means that if you're faced with an interviewee who provides short answers or sounds hesitant on the day of the webinar, the interviewee can simply use the transcription for support. Also, having rehearsed the webinar prior to the broadcast will allow you to put together slides to illustrate the points made during the interview, making the whole experience more enjoyable for listeners.

CASE STUDY: STEVEN ESSA

After running my first few webinars successfully and profitably, I realized that in order to scale my results, all I needed was to get more people into my sales funnel/webinar. The strategies that other people suggested involved either costly online advertising (which I couldn't afford at the time) or list swapping (which I couldn't implement because I didn't have a big enough list to bargain with). Other strategies involved blogging, but that would have been too slow for the results I was after.

While attending an Internet marketing conference, I heard about the power of interviews for list building and sales— interviews with experts during which products could potentially be sold. I soon came up with the idea of running a 'seven experts, seven weeks' webinar series. In this series, I'd interview experts, build an audience for my own webinars, and generate income from promoting their products as an affiliate during the interview.

I approached Internet marketing experts at events and through my own network. A few turned me down but a few accepted the offer! I used gotowebinar.com to record the interviews and create registration pages to collect registrants' contact details. I then promoted the interviews to my own Facebook and Twitter network, as well as to my own small email database of 50 people. I invited everyone to share the registration link with their network.

By the third week of running the weekly interviews, over 100 people had registered. I used that small list to promote my own webinar, and made over $10,000 in sales. After the seven-week series ended, I'd built a list of over 700 people who knew me, liked me and trusted me. This became a key weapon for future sales generation. The best part of it all is that I built very good business relationships with the experts I interviewed, and built my credibility in that industry twice as fast.

I signed up to a service for $200 a month, where I'd be booked as an interviewee on podcast shows almost every week. During the podcast show, the podcast host would interview me on my knowledge about webinars and digital marketing. Usually, at the end of a podcast interview, the host would ask the question: "Where can people find out more about you?" That's where I'd redirect them to my 90-minute webinar, where I'd explain and demonstrate the power of webinars and then offer my "Webinar Magic" home study course for $2,997.

I started to attract new customers as a result of being interviewed on podcasts, and success stories from people who had implemented my tips started coming in. Joshua Smith from Arizona, for example, a business owner who runs a real estate company, a software company and a coaching company listened to one of my podcast interviews. He later got in touch with me directly, saying, "After following to a T the tips shared, I ran a product launch using webinars which brought in $104,000 in revenue, for a product that hadn't been created yet."

MONEY ON DEMAND

CHAPTER 13

WEB TV

According to recent studies, watching TV online is growing extremely fast. Adobe's recent study showed that total TV viewing over the Internet recently grew by 388 per cent! Some think that web television will soon become the only television.

Regardless of whether this will eventuate, the reasons behind the rapidly growing trend towards web television are:

1. There is more unique content. Unique videos, serving the needs of micro-niches, are now available online
2. Internet speeds have dramatically increased and made the process of uploading and watching video on the web much easier and faster
3. The ability to watch web content from any device, such as a smart phone or tablet. The larger screen smart phone could soon become the device of choice for web TV consumption
4. The flexibility it provides, by allowing consumers to watch anytime and anywhere—allowing the consumer to have total control of their viewing experience

What makes web TV such a powerful Money-On-Demand strategy, is that anyone can now produce broadcast-quality content at very little cost from their own living room. You no longer need expensive and complex equipment such as lighting, microphones and sophisticated cameras. In fact, some very effective commercials have been shot on a smart phone. Smart phones even allow you to edit your recording without having to rely on external editing software.

Producing a web TV show can be very easy and fast. People often make the mistake of thinking that you need a studio and a lot of time to handle post-production. In reality, you could produce 12 web TV shows, enough to cover three months of content, in a single afternoon. All that is required is a bit of planning.

The key when committing to a show is consistency. You need to be consistent in terms of delivery, format, length, delivery style (formal or informal – live or pre-recorded), and broadcast time and day. The best practice is to deliver your show on a daily, weekly or monthly basis, with a consistent brand that connects with your target audience.

There are many benefits to running your own web TV show:

- The opportunity for you and your business to stand out by doing something unusual. When you run your own web TV show, you automatically position yourself as an expert and authority figure in your market and make more people want to buy from you.
- The consistent creation of unique, quality content that can be repurposed and re-used under different formats. For example, a web TV episode can be turned into a podcast, a Vodcast, a blog post, an article, a YouTube video, a newsletter, etc....
- Having a web TV show opens many direct and indirect monetization opportunities.
    o Direct: Each episode can end with an ad for your product.

- o Direct: You can sell advertising space once the show becomes big enough to appeal to advertisers or sponsors.
- o Indirect: List building. The database collected from viewers and listeners can be used for marketing via email, SMS or direct mail.
- o Indirect: Each episode can generate a lot of traffic to your other business touch points such as your website, blog and main sales funnel.
- o Indirect: Increase in joint venture opportunities. You can use episodes to endorse another business, brand or product in exchange for that business doing the same for you. This can become a very effective traffic, leads and sales generation technique.

Episodes do not have to be long. Very effective web TV shows are usually no longer than 20 to 30 minutes. In fact, they can be as short as five minutes, as long as they deliver the promised value.

The key when implementing the Money-On-Demand Web TV strategy is to be generous with your time and content and serve your audience in a way that nobody else can match. When you offer value for free consistently, you'll have earned prospects' interest instead of buying it. Eventually, you'll no longer have to rely on complex and expensive marketing strategies to sell your products, because customers will be flooding your way.

Web TV — Becoming the rock star of your own show

1. Choose your target market.
   Create your ideal prospect avatar: a profile description that includes demographic information such as age, marital status, gender and psychographics such as their habits, fears and challenges.

2. Decide on a name for your show.
   The name should be available across different channels, such as on Facebook and YouTube, and even as a hashtag if possible. It should be short (three words maximum) and easy to remember and spell.

3. Decide on the format. You'll have to decide on:

   a. The length of each episode
   b. The topics covered for at least three months' worth of episodes. Ideally, each topic should be the equivalent of one problem your target audience is facing or likely to face. Your web TV episode would help to solve that single problem.
   c. The delivery style (formal or informal). You could choose to have a casual approach and speak direct-to-camera from your desk, in a similar style to Gary Vaynerchuk's #AskGaryVee show. You could record interviews and add visuals to the narration, or you could alternate between direct-to-camera and slides as we do on our video blog: socialmediaworldwide.com/blog.

STEVEN AND CORINNA ESSA

d. The setting (office space, studio background, outdoor setting, etc....).
e. Whether it will be available only as a recording or as a live broadcast.
f. What purpose the web TV show will serve (which direct or indirect monetization method will be applied).

4. Schedule the show.
   Schedule days for:
   a. Scripting the show
   b. Recording the episodes
   c. Editing them (This applies only if your show is available only as a recording. Should you decide to initially broadcast the show live and make the recording available only after it's been broadcast live, you'll have to plan the live broadcast time and dates.)

5. Script the show
   In order to minimize the time spent on post-production, script the content as much as possible. When the content is scripted, and you use a teleprompter, this can save hours and hours of editing later.
   If your web TV episode has a guest, plan the interview beforehand. Have pre-written questions and rehearse the interview if possible. This will also save a lot of time during post-production. We allow a full day for the research and scripting of twelve episodes.

6. Produce the show
   Producing the show involves recording the content. Depending on the length of the episodes, we allow a full day, sometimes two days, to record them all.

7. Post production
   Post production involves editing the recordings. Depending on the length of the episodes, we allow a full day or two for editing all the episodes.

8. Distribution
   You want to make your show available on as many platforms as possible and in as many formats as possible:
   - Here are some popular video submission websites:
     o Youtube.com
     o Vimeo.com
     o Dailymotion.com
     o Blip.tv
     o ITunes
   - Social networking sites:
     o Facebook.com
     o Twitter.com
     o Instagram.com
     o Linkedin.com
   - If you decide to create an audio version of your show, your web TV show can also become an online radio show through tools such as stitcher.com.

9. Marketing.
   In line with the 80/20 marketing rule, 20 per cent of your time should be spent producing the shows and 80 per cent should be spent marketing them. Promoting your web TV show can be as simple as emailing your existing database and inviting them to share the show. You can reward your audience through giveaways and bonuses for promoting your show to *their* audience. Alternatively, you can buy

advertising space from networks such as Twitter.com, Facebook.com, Linkedin.com and Instagram.com as well as from solo ad providers such as udimi.com.

CASE STUDY: ANDREW LOCK

Andrew Lock is an Internet marketer, entrepreneur and host of the Web TV show *Help My Business*. He uses the Money-On-Demand Web TV strategy both to build a following and nurture his list by providing a free, weekly, 20-minute show. The show provides practical marketing tips, big business lessons from well-known brands, and numerous little-known online resources that small business owners can use to grow their business. It also answers questions submitted by viewers.

The show has been running since 2008, and in 2009 became the number one most popular marketing web TV show in the Apple iTunes store, beating well-known 'traditional business training' shows.

Andrew monetizes his show by having sponsors who are mentioned on the show and on the show's website. He also promotes events, products and books and includes links to these items in the 'resources' section on his website.

Lastly, to build his audience further and benefit from word of mouth, he gives away a free .pdf book in exchange for sharing the show on social media.

CHAPTER 14

TELE-SUMMIT

A tele-summit is one of the most powerful business-building tactics. Although it requires a lot of work upfront, the work you put in initially will pay off for years to come— directly, in terms of sales, and indirectly, in terms of your reputation, authority in your industry, quality of relationships built, brand awareness, lead-generation, traffic generation and content curation.

A tele-summit is an online event, either broadcast live or pre-recorded, in which speakers and experts deliver their presentations on a specific topic. Tele-summits usually run for a few days and are hosted by a single person who is responsible for the smooth running of the event and for introducing or interviewing each expert.

Tele-summits — The art of leveraging success

1. Planning
   This is the most important part of the process.
   When planning, you must decide on the following:
   - The topic
   - The format
   - The length
   - The speakers
   - The monetization strategy

- The finer details of the execution process such as the tools required to implement the plan

2. Building the team
   Like any other project, a tele-summit requires a team of people responsible for specific tasks.
   Ideally, the team should comprise:
   - The host, who is responsible for:
     o Liaising with speakers
     o Interviewing and recording the presentations or interviews
     o Marketing the event
   - A web developer who is responsible for:
     o Putting together the website for the tele-summit
     o Designing the funnels
     o Uploading the recordings onto the website
   - A video or audio editor who is responsible for:
     o Editing the marketing material
     o Editing the interviews
   - A graphic designer who is responsible for:
     o Designing the branding
     o Creating the logo
     o Sourcing the images needed
     o Designing the marketing material
   - A copywriter who is responsible for writing compelling copy for:
     o Sales letters
     o Lead capture pages
     o Sales videos
     o Ads
     o Website
   - An assistant who is responsible for:
     o Administrative tasks
     o Email support

o Phone support

3. Inviting speakers
The judicious selection of speakers is what can make or break a tele-summit. Just like any other event, the panel should include at least one speaker who acts as a draw-card. Ideally, every speaker should have a reputation that would attract a large audience. However, securing at least one celebrity expert for the panel won't only attract a large audience with minimal marketing efforts, but will also entice other speakers of the same caliber to participate.

The key to inviting speakers is to underline the benefits for them of being part of your event (such as increased exposure and brand awareness).

Never ask speakers to complete too many tasks. Don't ask them to write and broadcast emails to their list to promote the event, publish social media posts, provide their biography, their picture or any other special requirements you may have. These tasks may mean that time-poor experts won't want to participate.

Only ask for 30 to 40 minutes of their time to record the presentation or interview. First, research the information you need from them (such as their profile picture or their biography) on their website or other websites they've been featured on. This will limit the material that interviewees have to submit.

You can, of course, ask a speaker to promote the tele-summit in any way they can or are willing to, but this should definitely not be a pre-requisite.

If they agree to promote your event, provide them with ready-made marketing material such as banner ads, social media posts, images and email marketing copy. This will further increase your chances of them delivering on their promise.

4. Marketing and launching
Launching a tele-summit usually consists of three phases:
   • Phase one: Announcing the tele-summit and inviting people to join the guest list
   • Phase two: Marketing the tele-summit while it's taking place
   • Phase three: Marketing the tele-summit after it has been completed

Each phase should be marketed to the same extent, but the approach for each phase is different.

Phase one should focus mainly on 'the promise'. You must promise an extraordinary event where groundbreaking information will be revealed to the few smart people who were fast enough to secure their place. It should be evident in the marketing material of phase one that the secrets revealed and information shared is unlikely to be found anywhere else except for the summit.

Phase two should include some of the secrets already revealed by the experts, as proof of the value of attending the summit. It should also contain testimonials from attendees, which act as 'social proof'. Ideally, the biggest draw-cards of the event should appear towards the end of the summit to keep the momentum up and to leverage their name in the marketing material of phase two.

Phase three is an opportunity to build the audience even further by leveraging the contacts of the attendees. You market access to the recordings to registrants, as an opportunity for them to catch anything they may have missed or wish to go over again. When you do, it's a massive opportunity for registrants to share the summit with their own audience via social media.

Considering that most people have an average of 140 contacts on each social network they belong to, so invite them in an email to "tweet" about their experience of the summit. This will put the marketing process of phase three on steroids.

5. Monetizing
    There are direct and indirect ways to monetize a tele-summit.
    - Direct: Sell tickets. Prices of tickets can vary from $47 to a few hundred dollars depending on the subject, the industry and the exclusivity of the content.
    - Direct: Sell products at the end of each presentation. If the product belongs to the expert, a simple affiliate agreement would allow the host to benefit from a portion of the sales generated.
    - Direct: Tele-summit hosts may decide after the event to close free access and either sell the recordings for a one-off fee or place the recordings in a password-protected membership site, and charge a monthly access fee.
    - Direct: Recruit sponsors for the tele-summit. This would allow you to make the tele-summit

a sell-free zone while still monetizing the event.

- Indirect: A tele-summit can be used as a database builder so that you can send email marketing campaigns, direct mail marketing campaigns and SMS marketing campaigns to your own list. The list you build can bring you revenue for life. Also, owning a database may open doors to further joint venture opportunities and therefore more exposure, traffic, leads and sales. A mailing list that has been nurtured and updated regularly can be rented or even sold to advertisers and marketers, bringing in further revenue.

- Indirect: Use the content shared during the tele-summit as a website traffic generator. Sections of the content can be repurposed either in a text-based, video or audio format and submitted to traffic-generation platforms such as YouTube or blogs. Giving free access to sections of the content will entice people to purchase access to the entire recording.

- Indirect: The content created in different formats can allow you to advertise products and services. For example, certain topics could be transcribed and turned into a blog post, which could include links or banner ads to your sales funnel.

- Indirect: Hosting a tele-summit makes you a household name and authority figure in your industry, and therefore you can attract high-paying clients or a higher volume of sales, much faster.

- Indirect: Building key relationships. It's hard to measure the return on investment of having key contacts and relationships with "important" people. However, there are many possibilities to monetize these contacts. You could ask them, for example, to endorse your product or become a sponsor for your next event.

CASE STUDY: ANTHONY TRAN

Anthony Tran is the founder of the *Marketing Access Pass* podcast, and host of the *Traffic Generation All Stars* tele-summit. His tele-summit ran for eight days, and had 24 experts sharing their unique strategies for generating traffic online.

The format was simple: he interviewed all experts on Skype and then submitted three interviews a day on separate web pages, using a lead-capture page builder.

Access to the summit was free, and this allowed him to build a database of 1,600 new people within a few days. Considering that an email subscriber is usually worth $1 a month (provided subscribers are emailed regularly with a combination of free and paid offers) a database of 1,600 people would naturally result in a monthly revenue of $1,600 as a result of email marketing campaigns.

To market the event, he used his existing podcast, blog and social media presence and used paid social media ads for more reach. His landing pages converted at an average of 30 per cent, and every lead generated using paid advertising cost an average of $2.50.

Although the tele-summit was free for those watching the broadcast at the scheduled date and time, he secured an affiliate agreement with some speakers who used the platform to sell their products. He also sold access to the recordings at $97 during the week of the tele-summit to people who couldn't make it at the specified time. Afterwards, he turned his tele-summit into an information product, which sold at $197.

However, the key relationships he built through that summit will pay off for years to come, and have enabled him to put himself on the map when it comes to digital marketing. He admits that most of the experts featured on his tele-summit now have an 'I'll do anything for you' attitude towards him—which is priceless.

CHAPTER 15

PRODUCT PLACEMENT

When people first think of 'product placement' or sponsorships they think of companies paying thousands of dollars to have their logo placed at local events, desperately trying to get a piece of the action. With the advent of high quality, content-rich webinars, publishers (webinar hosts) can now connect with advertisers to offer sponsorship packages. In turn, advertisers can experience higher and more tangible results than when using more traditional advertising methods. This method has become an increasingly attractive alternative for advertisers.

Sponsorship packages can vary between $10,000 and $50,000 for a single webinar; hence they can be a serious source of revenue for webinar hosts and they are quite easy to secure.

The benefit of using the Money-On-Demand Product Placement strategy, is guaranteed income upfront—enough to cover marketing and production costs while still experiencing high profit margins. Advertisers, by sponsoring webinars, are given the opportunity to:

- Raise their brand awareness over a period of weeks and months
- Provide education to their audience
- Generate a list of named prospects

Product Placement —
Untapped income sources

1. Carefully design the sponsorship packages.
   When you put together the different levels of sponsorship packages, make sure that they each emphasize not only the 60- or 90-minute webinar, but also the whole campaign: pre-webinar, webinar and post webinar, in order for the sponsor to understand the multiple lead-generation opportunities.

   - During the pre-webinar period, when efforts are being made to secure registrants, sponsors should be featured in all marketing materials. Marketing materials could include:
     o Blog posts, discussing the topic covered in the upcoming webinar, with a link or multiple links redirecting to the sponsor.
     o An email newsletter announcing the webinar, while also including the sponsor's branding and potentially clickable links to their touch points.
     o Video marketing. Video invitations to webinars tend to have a higher registration rate and also add value to sponsorship packages.
     o A webinar invitation by a direct mail letter.
     o A tab on your website for 'upcoming webinars' which redirects to the registration page and features the sponsor prominently.
     o A registration confirmation email sent out to registrants to provide access

details to the webinar, is also an effective place to mention the sponsor.

- o If you choose to provide downloadable .pdf resources or any supporting material prior to the webinar, links to the sponsor can be included.

- During the broadcast of the webinar, there are three opportunities to mention the sponsor:
  - o Discreetly on the slides themselves.
  - o At the start of the webinar, where the host would state, "Today's webinar is brought to you by XYZ" followed by a short description of the sponsor.
  - o In the middle of the webinar, as a 'commercial break.' 30 seconds to one minute should suffice as a commercial break.

- The post-webinar period is also a very effective time to mention sponsors.
  - o A 'thank-you for attending' email could include information linking back to the sponsor.
  - o Post-webinar marketing could include an email with the replay link and a mention of the sponsor.
  - o If you produce and distribute a DVD of the webinar recording, the packaging could also mention the sponsor.

2. Price the sponsorship packages

A good process to follow is to offer a menu with three choices, such as 'silver partner', 'gold partner' and 'platinum partner' packages. Prices will be based on the value each package brings and the level of guarantee you can provide.

For example, if each sales-lead were worth $500 to a sponsor, offering a 'silver partner' package at $10,000 would mean you'd have to prove that generating a minimum of 20 sales-leads would be achieved. As each sponsorship package increases in price, so should the value offered.

For example,
- The silver package could include:
  - Mentioning the sponsor in all pre-marketing materials
  - Mentioning the sponsor once on the webinar
  - A certain number of sales-leads guaranteed
- The gold package could include:
  - Mentioning the sponsor in all pre-marketing materials
  - Mentioning the sponsor three times on the webinar
  - A higher number of sales-leads guaranteed
- The platinum package could include:
  - Mentioning the sponsor during all three phases
  - Guaranteeing a higher number of sales-leads compared to the silver and gold package

Although not all sponsorship packages offer any sales-lead guarantees, if guarantees are provided where the sponsor can clearly see his risk is very small or non-existent, securing partners will become almost effortless.

If you decide to remove any guarantees, make sure you emphasize tangible results in your pitch, such as "exposure to 60,000 targeted prospects". A potential sponsor would then calculate how much such exposure would usually cost him by making comparisons with previous advertising expenditure, and would most likely agree to the deal if your offer were competitive.

3. Research your prospective sponsors
When looking for sponsors, the 80/20 rule applies. 80 per cent of your time should be spent on research and preparation and 20 per cent on selling.

When conducting research, look for information about the potential sponsor's advertising budgets and previous advertising expenditures, as well as the value of a lead and the value of a customer for them. This will enable you to price packages accordingly and sell these packages more easily.

Up to six months should be allowed for the research and preparation phase and the information collected should include:
- A list of potential sponsors
- Their advertising budgets
- The contact details of the decision maker
- Details of previous sponsorship packages purchased
- Their 'why' (what are their needs and wants and their bigger goals)
- What their competition is doing
- A clear idea about their demographic

- A description of the sponsor's target audience

The time dedicated to research and preparation will allow you to design your packages according to the potential sponsors' needs. If you shape proposals based on your own needs, this makes closing the sale very difficult.

Once you have a shortlist of prospects, the effort you put into relationship building will pay off in terms of gathering information about them. If you can connect on a personal level with the decision maker, this will increase your chances of closing the deal.

4. Design the customised proposal
   The proposal should follow a certain format, and include standard sections and specific sponsorship-related language. Give the proposal to someone who has experience in closing sponsorship deals to ensure it's a winner.

   A proposal should include:
   - A description of what you do
   - Your story or your company's story (to make an emotional connection and stand out from other sponsorship offers)
   - The benefits of becoming your sponsor (based on their needs and wants). Salespeople often think that the more benefits they list, the more likely they're to convince the prospect to buy, but this can backfire if the benefits mentioned don't apply to the sponsor.
   - A description of your demographics (so the prospect realizes your audience is a perfect match with theirs)

- A description of the team or board of advisors (making it obvious they're dealing with experienced A-players)
- A price list, as prospects tend to ignore those that don't have one

5. Close the deal
   This job should be given to an experienced B2B sales person. There is nothing worse than handing the responsibility of deal-closing to 'conversationalists' (as the late Zig Ziglar called them), or 'order takers' instead of real sales people who really get to work as soon as they hear "no".

   Make an appointment for them with the decision maker, to take along your great sponsorship proposal based on the sponsor's needs and wants.

   A good sales person should:
   - Be aware of what the potential objections could be, and have a clear plan about how to answer them effectively.
   - Find out what kind of person they'll be dealing with.
   - Know that each person is different, and therefore each proposal needs to be sold differently.
   - Be a very good chameleon to adapt to their prospect's personality.
   - Position themselves as a problem solver rather than a sales person.
   - Be a good listener.
   - Have done their research.
   - Align themselves with the prospect's needs and wants.

- Be confident that the sponsorship packages will deliver guaranteed tangible results.
- Back up their case with proof (with the help of past webinar reports and testimonials).
- Make comparisons with what they're already spending on other marketing efforts and underline how the option on offer is a smarter one.

CASE STUDY: ANTHONY CHADWICK

Anthony Chadwick, a dermatology vet from the UK, met me at an Internet conference in the UK. At the time, Anthony was a busy vet who finished work everyday at 7 pm, and then, some nights, had to rush out for an 8pm meeting, 40 minutes drive away. He had no choice, as these meetings were compulsory to keep up with his CPD (continued professional development) points.

When I introduced him to the idea of webinars he wanted to use them to provide training to vets. He joined my "Webinar Magic" home study course and presented his first webinar in March 2010 with hundreds of people registered to watch it. Soon after, he sold his practice and webinars became his 'bread and butter'. His company, *The Webinar Vet* specializes in providing expert, topical and varied CPD for busy vets and veterinary practices via webinar.

Anthony has enjoyed a steady growth of members, both European and international, and now has over 200 hours of archive material available, as well as weekly live broadcasts. Aside from monetizing his webinars by selling them individually for a few hundred British pounds, and selling monthly memberships to the webinars for 47 British pounds, Anthony also monetizes the content with sponsors.

His sponsors are usually extremely relevant to the topic covered in the webinar. For example, he ran a webinar titled *Orthopaedic expertise series* sponsored by Orthomed, a leading provider of surgical instruments. References to sponsors are usually made on the banner ad promoting the webinar, on the home page of his website, and during the webinar.

CHAPTER 16

LICENSING

Licensing has been used increasingly over the last 30 years as a marketing and brand extension tool, as well as an additional revenue stream. It has been a business model used by some of the world's richest people. Donald Trump, for example, created the remarkable Trump brand and licensed it. In fact, Donald Trump doesn't own most of his properties. Instead, he licenses his name to property developers and offers property management services. In Manhattan for example, 17 properties hold his name, but he only owns five of them outright, according to Forbes.

When well executed, a strong licensing relationship benefits both the licensor and the licensee. Each has their own goals and aims that ultimately add value to both the product or service, and the consumer.

Typically, a licensee will lease the right to someone else's product. They can then:
- Incorporate the product into their own products (to add value to them)
- Sell the product as a stand-alone item but not share ownership in the product

A licensee must adhere to the licensing agreement, market the product, and pay the royalties.

The licensor gives the licensee:

- The right to use the product
- Timely approvals when necessary
- Guidance about the brand, the product, the packaging and the promotional material
- Assistance in selling the product

When many licenses have been sold, licensors will typically hire licensing agents to manage their licensees who will assume duties such as contract negotiations, timely payments and approval processes.

If you own a webinar-related business, licensing your webinars should be your ultimate goal. The returns can be huge for the little work that is involved.

However, the success of the Money-On-Demand Licensing strategy will depend upon the strength of your initial product or service. With this model, having a good product or service idea is not enough. The idea must be exceptional. The webinar should convert at a minimum of ten per cent to be appealing enough to license.

As a licensor of a webinar-related product, you're responsible for updating the product regularly, as information products can quickly become outdated. In addition, your brand and name should have an impeccable reputation, as potential licensors are quick to do their due diligence. A single bad review or online conversations from disgruntled customers can turn away potential licensors.

Your business systems and processes—from marketing to customer acquisition and product delivery—should be running smoothly and efficiently. This is because licensees not only buy the rights to sell your product, they also, ultimately, buy your systems and processes. Systems and processes include marketing material, Customer Relations

Management (CRM) systems, staff contracts, sales scripts, and business templates (such as good performing sales funnels and ads).

The benefits for a webinar business owner to license his product include:

- Eliminating marketing costs associated with selling the webinar product
- Being paid ongoing royalties which translate into direct profits
- An added revenue stream for the core business from the license upfront fees
- An increase in product sales
- Increased exposure in new channels
- Product control and control over brand image (a webinar business owner will profit from their creative efforts while maintaining control over how they're sold and used)
- Business development with relatively small upfront risk (by licensing a product, a business owner can move into new countries and new markets with a smaller upfront investment, than by building and staffing their own operation)
- Reduction in in-house costs related to hiring and managing staff to sell and/or produce more products

The benefits for a licensee to own a license to a webinar product include:

1. Taking advantage of all the brand building and image building that exists (it can take thousands of dollars and sometimes millions of dollars to build a brand from scratch)
2. Adding another product to their line without having to go through the process of product creation

3. Holding the blueprint of a proven income generating system without having to go through the process of creating and testing a product and the risk it involves in terms of investment
4. Saving time in having to create and market a product with no guarantee of success
5. Tapping into the licensor's expertise, network and experience

As the licensor of a webinar-related product, you can experience excellent returns on your investment, both in time and money, while doing relatively little work for it. If you sell 15 licenses a year at $15,000 each, for example, that could bring in an added revenue stream of $225,000 a year.

In addition, should each licensee generate $10,000 a month in sales, and the fees are five per cent of the gross sales, the licensor would also have an extra $7,500 recurring monthly income from royalties paid by the 15 licensees ($500 x 15 licensees).

Once you've invested time and effort into your webinar product and streamlined your processes to make it license worthy—from marketing to customer acquisition and product delivery—licensing will give you considerable returns.

Licensing alleviates the pressure of having to generate sales in-house and frees up your time to pursue other things. It also gives you the quickest path to far-reaching distribution—when your product is in the hands of the right licensors— with little effort and risk.

Licensing — Ultimate freedom formula

1. Make a licensing webinar
   Have a carefully crafted webinar with a title that underlines the benefit of owning a license. We've sold licenses of our social media management company from a single webinar.

   If the earning potential of owning a license is $10,000 a month based on the numbers from the current business, a webinar to sell the license could be titled, *How to earn $10,000 a month thanks to XYZ*. The webinar would teach in five steps how to run a $10,000 a month business. It would then offer licenses to an already existing and proven system that generates $10,000 a month.

2. Sell the license
   Selling the license to the product should be the natural progression of the webinar and represent a fast opportunity for making $10,000 a month by following a proven system.

   You should be as skilled at selling the business as you are at selling the product.

   A licensing agent or licensing firm can help you with everything from contract negotiations to license development and packaging, and ensure the resell license is a win-win proposition for both the licensor and the licensee.

CASE STUDY: CORINNA ESSA

When Corinna began her journey as an information marketer, she sold hundreds of copies of her *How to make $700 a week thanks to Twitter* online home study course.

Her webinar was converting at a steady ten per cent— often more.

A few years ago, while I was delivering a workshop to a group of eight people in Perth, I decided to broadcast Corinna's webinar live on Twitter to show the audience how to run live webinars and also educate them about the power of Twitter. The webinar was promoting a Twitter marketing home study course so after the webinar, I surveyed the people who had decided not to purchase the product to find out what was missing from the offer. A few said they really enjoyed the webinar but were too time-poor to study and implement a new course—they'd rather purchase a done-for-you service.

This gave us the idea of launching a social media marketing company, which now helps hundreds of businesses around the world leverage the power of social media without them having to do any of the legwork.

Shortly after the company was launched, it became over-subscribed. So one of the strategies we decided to pursue was Licensing, where we'd sell licenses to sell the service.

The company was generating thousands of dollars a month and had high profit margins, so we titled the webinar to sell licenses: *How to make $10,000 a month in 2 hours a day thanks to social media management.*

The webinar presentation was structured into the following steps:

Step 1: Package your social media services
Step 2: Build and train a team of social media managers
Step 3: Drive traffic to your webinar to attract customers
Step 4: Joint venture to accelerate your success
Step 5: Manage the business in two hours a day

The webinar offered the opportunity for people to understand the business model and make an informed decision on whether owning a license to the business would be of benefit to them.

The social media management license package sold at $15,000 and included:

- The right to the webinar itself, which was selling the social media service and converting at ten per cent
- A ready-made website displaying all prices and services together with the testimonials
- Staff training manuals
- Video tutorials
- Email marketing and online advertising templates to market the service
- Customer follow-up emails
- Sales training
- Branding and graphic design
- A detailed description of the end-to-end process of running a social media management company

Selling a $15,000 license on a webinar is not a lincar process, wherein a prospect watches the webinar and then 60 minutes later parts with $15,000—so the sales process had to be broken down into three steps.

1. The prospect paid a $1,000 refundable deposit as an 'expression of interest'
2. The licensor interviewed the prospect to ensure that they qualified as a licensee.
3. At the end of the interview, the $1,000 deposit was refunded if the applicant didn't qualify, or the remaining $14,000 was invoiced if the prospect passed the interview process.

WHERE TO NOW?

I'm sure that, by now, you realize there are many, many ways to generate a full-time income from home— in just a few hours a week—thanks to webinars. And you don't need many resources to apply any of the strategies shared in this book. All it takes is access to a computer, an Internet connection, and a willingness to follow one of the many income generation strategies laid out in this book.

The Money-On-Demand: Show-And-Tell strategy in chapter one is a very effective way to leverage your own knowledge, experience and products (if you already have products).

The Money-On-Demand: JV and Partnership strategy in chapter two is a fantastic way of leveraging your existing contacts and marketing skills while profiting from other people's webinars.

The Money-On-Demand: Lazy Money strategy in chapter three proves that the sales process can be easily automated, and it only takes a single bout of hard work.

The Money-On-Demand: Partnership strategy, described in chapter four, has been responsible for taking our million-dollar company to a multi-million-dollar company. It's a fantastic new way for people to scale their business using their existing brand, customers, and contacts without necessarily working harder, hiring more staff or spending more.

The Money-On-Demand: Webinar Facilitation strategy demonstrates that with the skills learnt in chapter five you could have multiple income streams without ever having to build a mailing list, generate traffic or present a webinar. Instead, you're simply leveraging other experts' knowledge and contacts while helping them grow their business.

The Money-On-Demand: Affiliate strategy in chapter six proves that even if you don't have a product to sell, and don't want to create one or deliver one, it won't stop you from being able to generate a full-time income from webinars.

The Money-On-Demand: Paid Webinar strategy in chapter seven shows how easy it is for anyone to create a high-end product thanks to webinars, and anyone can put together a product easily without having any up-front costs or stock.

The Money-On-Demand: Loop strategy in chapter eight is another webinar monetization strategy that allows anyone to generate monthly residual income, and leverage your knowledge for years to come.

The Money-On-Demand: JV Broker strategy in chapter nine is particularly lucrative for networkers looking to monetize the business relationships they've built without ever having to present a webinar, create a product or market anything.

The Money-On-Demand: Productization strategy in chapter ten proves how easy it is for anyone starting from scratch and without a product to sell, to put together and sell a high-end offer using webinars. In fact, this method has been responsible for generating six- and seven-figure incomes for complete webinar novices.

The Money-On-Demand: B2B strategy in chapter eleven is perfect for leveraging contacts with decision-makers and will soon become a recognized career. In fact, in some industries, having a B2B facilitator could become a necessity rather than a luxury.

The Money-On-Demand: Interview strategy in chapter twelve proves that conducting simple conversations on webinars can lead to a very lucrative business with the potential of making anyone become the 'Oprah Winfrey' of the Internet!

The Money-On-Demand: Web TV strategy in chapter thirteen is a fantastic new ongoing way to sell products while building a huge tribe of loyal fans.

The Money-On-Demand: Tele-summit method in chapter fourteen is another superb way to monetize webinars while becoming a celebrity in your niche and building a huge mailing list in a few weeks. In fact, by implementing the Tele-summit strategy, you'd be building an asset that could bring you revenue for years to come.

The Money-On-Demand: Product Placement strategy in chapter fifteen is perfect for people who don't enjoy selling, and a highly effective way to monetize webinars.

The Money-On-Demand: Licensing strategy in chapter sixteen proves that webinars can be bundled into high-profit products of their own and take you from owning a six-figure web business to owning a seven-figure business.

The choice is now yours. You can pick one or more of the Money-On-Demand strategies laid out in this book, and start your journey as a web entrepreneur. You can earn multiple income streams from home and solve many of life's common problems. Or, you can keep working hard, exchanging your time for money.

Sometimes it only takes one small, insignificant sacrifice to live a life of freedom, success and professional fulfillment.

Both Corinna and I experienced a very similar journey before we finally met each other. We both came from families that emphasized the importance of following a traditional education, learning a trade and getting a safe, secure job. But both Corinna and I had our dreams shattered as we discovered the myth of careers and the limitations that being in a job can impose on your life.

It was only when we decided to try something we were unfamiliar with, something that implied we'd have to sacrifice one weekend, that our lives changed.

My friend invited me to a weekend seminar on web marketing and although I was unwilling to spend my only free time during the week to attend a seminar, I pushed myself to go.

That seminar became a turning point in my life. I went from being half a million dollars in bad debt to multi-millionaire thanks to the information and tools shared that weekend.

Corinna went through a similar journey. Her brother strongly advised her to attend a web-business seminar in London. And although she was unemployed at the time, couldn't afford to spend money on airfares, and was skeptical about how the information shared could impact her life in any way, she made it to the seminar.

That weekend opened her eyes to the sea of opportunities and led her to building a multi-million-dollar web company.

When we look back at our journeys, we realize that all it took for us to live a life of freedom, success and significance was one sacrifice and the realization that we had nothing to lose. We feel confident that by reading this book you'll have the same realization.

If you enjoyed reading this book and appreciated the insights that it presented into how to create unprecedented wealth based on the skills, experiences and assets you already have, look out for the Money-On-Demand seminars coming to a city near you.

We believe that anyone willing to succeed and follow a proven Money-On-Demand system can change their path and live the life they always dreamed of living.

We trust that you'll join us on this journey and by your example, light the path to freedom and success for others to follow.

Start Making Money-On-Demand **Today** With Our **FREE** Webinar Software

You picked up this book, and you read it cover to cover. This means you're serious about using webinars to create your dream lifestyle.

To help you start building your web-entrepreneur empire as quickly as possible, we are giving away our coveted webinar software: "Webinar Speed"

You can download your free software here: x10effect.com/webinarspeed

Discovering the many ways you can make big money with webinars is the easy part. After all, you're not armed with the 16 fastest ways to become a millionaire online!

But setting up and profiting from your first webinar can be tricky...

Other webinar software tools are complicated to use, require technical know-how, and often don't provide you with accurate conversions statistics.

(And we would know because we've tried all of them!)

Plus, you need to set up a webinar landing page, a thank you page, process payments... the list goes on.

"Webinar Speed" handles the technical setup for you, so you can focus on what matters most: making sales.

Use our free software to save your time and get started cashing in on your first webinar right away. You can download it here: x10effect.com/webinarspeed

Now, the only question left for you to answer is: *which money-making webinar strategy will you try first?*

Printed in Great Britain
by Amazon

47711497R00127